MASTER KEY
TO
GOOD GOLF

BY

LESLIE KING

WORLD RENOWNED GOLF TEACHER

THE REVOLUTIONARY **"FREE ARM SWING"** METHOD.
THE ONLY TRUE SYSTEM APPROACH TO DEVELOPING A
SOUND-CONSISTANT GOLF SWING.

Exclusive North American Rights

Golf Associates
P.O. Box 2244
Menlo Park, Calif. 94025

Printed in U.S.A.

1st Printing, January 1980
2nd Printing, August 1981
3rd Printing, May 1984
4th Printing, February 1988

ISBN 0-9607140-0-6

Foreword
by Michael Bonallack
British Amateur Champion 1961, '65, '68, '69, '70

My only regret in having lessons from Leslie King is that I did not have them sooner.

From my very first visit I realised that here was a teacher who had only one way of teaching . . . no gimmicks . . . no modern fads . . . just a straightforward and uncomplicated way of consistently repeating an action to swing the club into the back of the ball and along the line of flight.

Each lesson concentrates on one aspect of the swing and each follows neatly and clearly on to the next. Thus, at the end a complete picture of the "model" exists in the mind of the pupil, and once this model is established it is always a comparatively easy task to correct errors if things start to go wrong.

With his new teaching manuals Leslie King has managed to put into print his complete method of swinging a golf club, and follows exactly the lessons he gives to all his pupils. I am sure they will be of great benefit to golfers of all ages and standards.

Michael. F. Bonallack

TABLE OF CONTENTS

Learning based upon a specific plan. An end to "trial and error" golf...

Although millions of people throughout the world play golf, very few indeed become really good golfers. Why is this?

I believe that the way in which the golf swing has been analysed is wrong, and consequently the teaching that is based upon this incorrect analysis is equally wrong. Incorrect teaching can never lead to progress and achievement.

In particular, I deplore the lack of "method", or "system", in the traditional way of teaching the golf swing. Golf teaching has tended to be a "try this", or "think about that" approach to problems. Nobody had made an attempt to clearly define what must happen in the golf swing, and then devise a clear teaching method to bring about the desired result.

Such a process has gone on in almost all other major sports in the world, with a consequence that standards have been raised all round. One has only to look at the remarkable level of attainment in Olympic and World track and field records over recent years as proof of that. This increase in performance levels is the result of improved teaching based upon correct study. Can golf really be the exception?

To make real progress in golf one must start from a correct analysis of the basic swing movement. Then, having discovered the essential principles, one must devise, and *test* a simple, clear-cut method of teaching those principles . . . a method that produces the desired result *each and every* time it is applied.

My life in golf has been devoted to this end. My "method" of teaching the golf swing has consistently produced International players, National and County Champions, single-figure players by the score, and most of all, it has provided a release from "trial and error golf" for thousands of "average players", as they are called. In fact, no player is "average". With correct training, even the most unlikely prospect can be turned into championship material. I know, because I have turned more than one 36 handicapper into an amateur of world class.

In view of such achievement, not just once, but year after year, I believe I can offer my method to any golfer, no matter what his standard, in the certain knowledge that by applying its principles he can realise his full potential in his chosen sport . . . and do so quite rapidly.

The Leslie King philosophy...

ACHIEVEMENT BY SYSTEMATIC TRAINING

Golf should be enjoyable. There is really no reason why a player should struggle on from year to year without improvement. But before it can become enjoyable and carefree, a player must go through an initial period of training in which he acquires what I term a "sound swing shape".

It's just like learning to ride a bicycle, driving a car, or learning how to play a musical instrument. During the learning process, movements are necessarily slow and deliberate and require great concentration. But as one progresses, the movements become instinctive and automatic, and you begin to enjoy the acquisition of the new skill. But your golf training, like these other activities, must be based upon a specific plan to be fruitful. Instructors who teach ballet, karate, horse riding, judo, or whatever, have a clear knowledge of what they are trying to create in their pupils, and an equally clear knowledge of the techniques that will take the pupil to the desired goal.

It should be the same in golf.

Actually, it is my belief that the golf swing is a precision movement that must be learned stage-by-stage, and that the game of golf is therefore more closely allied to ballet, the "martial arts" and gymnastics. These are activities in which absolute precision of movement is acquired by repetition of basic exercises and techniques. By constant repetition, sound technique is acquired . . . and becomes automatic . . . and artistry begins. That's what I mean by "method".

On a less elevated level, one can look to the technique of military rifle drill as an example of what I mean. In only three months a squad of unco-ordinated, indisciplined individuals is transformed into a smart body of men, capable of acting with consistency and timing, merely by repeating a defined series of movements until they become automatic and instinctive. The Drill Sergeant knows it can be done because he has done it before, and he demands absolute correctness from each man . . . not just something that approximates to correctness. The method he employs consistently achieves an end product.

It should be the same in golf. Unfortunately it isn't. Most golfers have absolutely no idea of what they are trying to achieve, and when they "practice" they merely build-in their faults. Golf instruction itself has tended to be a matter of "curing" this or that fault, rather than giving a player a defined programme for improvement. My "method" is just such a programme, and I have no doubt that by applying it, your game can *immediately* begin to improve. This is how it came into being.

THE SWING MODEL

As a young tournament player, I was searching, like all my contemporaries, for a consistent swing. I soon became aware that "traditional golf instruction" could not unlock the door to consistency. Indeed, it seemed to me that the concepts employed in traditional teaching were incorrect, and merely arrested progress. I decided then and there to carry out my own analysis of the golf swing completely independent of existing ideas, to see if I could unravel the mystery of the sound, consistent swing.

As I watched the top players in action I began to see the *same* distinctive "shape" emerging. There were minor variations in points of detail, admittedly, but in general, I recognised more or less the same "shape" each time I saw them swing . . . and they employed the same "shape" year after year. I had a "model" on which to base my studies.

The next task was to identify the features that went to make up the "model", and discover how they were achieved. I had completed my analysis by 1933/34, but I had been forced to conclusions about the swing which was nothing short of heresy then . . . and are even now considered to be quite revolutionary . . . although some of them have now been accepted as "standard technique".

Having analysed the sound swing movement, I then had to develop techniques for teaching it which would produce the desired results in pupils each and every time. This was a process of working with pupils and noting the *effect* that my words and concepts had upon their swings. In this way I discovered which concepts really produced the results that I was trying to achieve . . . and which did not, and gradually learning a way . . . a "method" . . . of communicating what I had learned so that I achieved consistency of result in my pupils.

Actually, I believe this process of testing concepts to prove that they produce the desired results is an obligation of every teacher or player who offers advice to others. It is simply not enough to express what you think or feel about the golf swing. You should be *sure* that the advice given, in the *form* that it is given, actually creates the result that you require . . . and does so consistently. One can only do this by face-to-face contact with pupils over a long period of time. In other words, this is, or should be, the specific skill of the experienced teacher, as opposed to the great player. It is in this area, I believe, that the instructional books of the world's greatest players have fallen down, and often done more harm than good. They express personal ideas rather than genuinely tested teaching concepts.

Just as a player is judged on his performance, a teacher

can only be judged by his results. If most of his pupils improve, he knows that he is on the right lines. If his pupils *sustain* this improvement, and if a number of them consistently move into the top ranks of amateur golf, the teacher can then confidently offer his knowledge to anyone . . . and do so with authority and belief in himself, no matter how unfasionable are his ideas.

I believe any golfer who goes to a teacher is *entitled,* because he pays well for the service, to see an improvement in his swing and in his score. If he does not, it is the teacher's responsibility . . . provided of course that the pupil has worked at what he has been told.

Further, a pupil is entitled to expect consistency of advice over a period of years. A teacher who "changes his tack" in the light of this or that "discovery" or "scientific fact" lacks real knowledge and should be avoided. I take pride in the fact that I have never failed to answer a pupil's question, and that my answer has been consistent with advice that I have given previously. Real knowledge is total. Half knowledge is fragmentary.

So we come back to "method". A teacher who does not work to a defined method cannot possibly have a clear idea of what he is trying to create in his pupil, and therefore cannot offer him a consistent and progressive programme of training. You cannot build a sound house if you do not have an equally sound plan.

I have often been criticised as "the man who teaches the same method to all golfers". In my book, this is the greatest compliment that could be paid to me, for nothing is worse than having no method at all. Indeed, this lack of systematic teaching is the very reason for the lack of standards in world golf instruction.

THE "SWING MODEL" TODAY

The model that I saw as a young man I have continued to see since, and I still see today in the swings of the greatest players. Indeed, I have had the singular pleasure of seeing that same model created in the swings of my own pupils to the point that they can be recognised as having a "King swing". The best examples of the model can be seen in the swings of Sam Snead, Max Faulkner, Tom Weiskopf, Gene Littler, Ben Hogan and Hale Irwin. These six men, I contend, are the best possible examples of a sound, consistent swing action which can hold up under the greatest pressure, and never vary.

My "method", I believe, creates the type of action that these men employ, although my method of conveying that action may differ markedly from the concepts that some of them have used to describe how they hit a golf ball.

Clearly, there are, and have been many great players who have employed highly individualistic styles, and are none the worse for it. In this category I would place Palmer, Trevino, Locke, Brewer and Barber, to name but a handful. But although these men apparently deviate from the "model", they do so only in the backswing. By the time the downswing begins they have "corrected" back to an orthodox "shape", and swing into and along the intended line of flight with a square blade, as do the others. I view their mannerisms as complications to their swings . . . but they are complications that are under *control.* But even these men who display individual characteristics in their swings *repeat* the same action each and every time they swing. So again, we have the application of a "method" . . . albeit an unorthodox one. Of one thing I am quite sure. It is the players who employ the simplest, most economical method who are the most consistent, and remain at the top longer than the rest.

These are the key words in golf. Soundness. Simplicity. Repetition. They all add up to CONSISTENCY . . . the name of this game.

Teaching the "Model"

So there it is . . . my concept of a "swing model". I teach the same movement to all golfers. There simply isn't one swing for pros and another swing for long handicappers. It is either sound or unsound. I strive to create the *same* end product in all of my pupils. They are taken, step by step, through all the stages of the "model", like building a structure, brick by brick. The end product is in my mind at all times, and each stage takes me closer to it. Thus, I can readily see each time a pupil comes to my school what stage he has reached. I don't have to ask him, and neither do my assistants. We do a team job . . . creating the same end product . . . and we all can therefore recognise precisely how much work has been done on each student.

We are not interested in temporary "cures" for hooks and slices. These are symptoms of an unsound swing, and we want to replace the bad action with a sound one. We are *positive.* Every student knows exactly what we want him to do, and as he achieves one phase, we move on to the next. Gradually, the entire swing takes place . . . a defined movement which is held by *repetition.* Soon, the player has an action that "sends the ball out there", dead straight, because it can't go anywhere else. That's what breeds confidence in one's swing . . . and performance arises out of confidence.

Eventually, the swing action is taken for granted . . . it is grooved and automatic. Then the student beings to play enjoyable, fluent golf, pitting his wits against the course, and par. And that's what golf is all about.

I have seen my method turn "duffers" into champions. I do not offer it to you in the hope that it may do you some good. If correctly followed and understood, I know it can do for you what it has done for countless Golfers over the years. So here's to better golf from now on . . . .

A free swing of the hands and arms, the basis of the golf action. A concept that must be grasped ...

My method of teaching the swing is based upon *a free swing of the hands and arms.* Just as a player freely swings his arms *from his shoulders* as he is walking down the fairway, he must learn to swing his hands and arms with *equal freedom and fluency* in his golf action.

There are several exercises at various stages of this Course which are designed to achieve this freedom of arm swing. Curiously enough, it has to be learned. The instinct of most golfers is to set the hands and arms in motion by *turning the body.* I believe the concept of "the one-piece takeaway" is responsible for this error. Be that as it may, I have observed that 99·9% of all new pupils who come to my School attempt to move the hands and arms (and therefore the club) with "body action". They simply do not realise that the arms *can* swing freely from the shoulder joints, *independent* of the body!

Thus, the first principle of the swing is this . . . THE GOLF ACTION IS BASED UPON A FREE SWING OF THE HANDS AND ARMS, INDEPENDENT OF THE BODY. THE BODY DOES NOT "PROPEL" (cause the movement of) THE HANDS AND ARMS AT ANY TIME.

In other words, a correct swing is based upon a free swing of the hands and arms. A bad swing is based upon "body propulsion" . . . an action in which the hands and arms are set in motion by body movement.

There is a profound difference between these two types of action, as you will see. Try to understand this concept right away. The sooner you grasp its meaning, the better for you.

What then is the correct role of the body in the swing? The role of the body is to *create the conditions* for this free, unrestricted swing of the hands and arms. If the body is correctly positioned at address, and thereafter is employed in a correct manner, a free swing of the hands and arms can take place. Conversely, if the body is out of position at the start, and is subsequently misused in the swing, the free swing of the hands and arms is *utterly destroyed,* and the whole action is wrecked.

In short, the body moves *in response* to what the hands and arms are doing. It is never responsible for creating *movement.* It has a *reactive* rather than a creative role.

This point can be illustrated in the following way. Think of a person about to crank the engine of a car with a starting handle. He first *positions* his feet and body, and then he applies force with his hand and arm. Again, a mechanic when working on an inaccessible part of the car engine first takes quite a bit of time to position his body so that he can *apply force with his hands.* In both cases, the body is being positioned to *enable* the hands to perform their task. A good body position permits *optimum* use of the hands. An awkward position *diminishes* the capacity of the hands to perform tasks.

It is just the same in the golf swing.

From this it follows that the body moves in a *quite specific way* in the golf swing. How it should move will be clearly defined at each stage as we go along. I term the learning of a correct body movement as "shaping the body" . . . that is, learning to use it in such a way that *promotes and assists* the free swing of the hands and arms, rather than inhibit this swing.

We will see that a free swing of the hands and arms, and the correct sequence of body movements upon which the former depends, result in a movement in which a swing into and along the intended line of flight occurs *automatically.* The swing is so "shaped" that the club cannot go anywhere *but squarely along the line of flight through impact.* Thus, I do not talk about "curing" hooks and slices. This is negative. Rather, I teach a swing movement in which the golfer is "programmed" as it were, to achieve a straight, powerful shot each and every time he swings.

Thus, we begin the process of building a new swing by *getting the basic posture correct.* By so doing, we *create the conditions* for a free swing of the hands and arms, and we also lay the foundation for *correct body movement* later on in the swing sequence.

So let's go . . .

The set-up

MASTER REFERENCE

I would ask you to pay particular attention to what I have to say about the set-up, and to study the drawings carefully. Check your position in front of a mirror often, as it is extremely easy to move out of position, and bad habits are developed quickly.

I really cannot stress too much the importance of a correct set-up. I have had to correct the position of many a top pro. and amateur as a preliminary to "cleaning up" the rest of the swing. All kinds of problems result from a poor set-up, and incredibly, few players ever look to the set-up as a possible source of error.

First, there is absolutely no tension in the set-up whatsoever. Quite the reverse. The set-up is basically an arrangement of the body which permits a free swing of the hands, arms and club. No more . . . no less.

Note the word *swing*. I will be stressing it again and again throughout this course of instruction. I will insist throughout that we swing the club . . . not *hit* the ball.

It is important to differentiate between "swinging" and "hitting" right from the start. I will have a great deal more to say about this at the appropriate time, but for the moment just remember that we are discussing the golf "swing" . . . and make it a swing.

When a new pupil comes to my School, I can tell from his set-up whether he appreciates the vital difference between "swinging" and "hitting." A "hitter" often takes a ham-fisted grip on the club, and his set-up immediately betrays his habit of relying upon the muscles of the body (particularly the shoulders) to set the club in motion. He often grimaces, clenches his teeth, and stiffens his arms and hands prior to moving the club. All of these symptoms are the first sure signs of a body heaver.

He is simply making life difficult for himself. It is quite impossible to achieve a correct backswing and downswing if the body is employed to move the club.

I first remind such a player that his arms have the capacity to swing! When walking down a fairway, he probably swings his arms beautifully. Unfortunately, when he reaches his ball he uses his body to move his hands and arms . . . and the club!

The purpose of the set-up is simply to arrange the body for a FREE SWING of the hands and arms··· particularly the LEFT hand and arm.
The body is balanced, active and live at all times ···anticipating movement.

These are your "Master Reference Illustrations" for the set-up. If ever you are in any doubt about your set-up position refer to these illustrations and check your position in a mirror.

Refer to your "Set-up Check Sheets" pages 31-38 while you're studying these illustrations.

The set up should anticipate the swing of the hands and arms

I am going to ask you to swing your hands and arms . . . particularly the left hand and arm . . . as the foundation of your golf swing.

The body does not turn to cause the arms to move. Rather, the body merely responds to a movement which has been started by the swing of the hands and arms.

This is a vitally important concept. You really must grasp this idea if you are ever to develop a reliable swing action. Please think about it and understand it.

THE HANDS AND ARMS ALONE START THE CLUB-HEAD MOVING BACK FROM THE BALL. THE SHOULDERS THEN RESPOND TO THIS MOVEMENT BY TURNING, TO ALLOW THE HAND AND ARM SWING TO PROGRESS TO THE TOP.

The purpose of the set-up is simply to arrange the body for this swing of the hands and arms. A bad set-up impedes this swing . . . or even renders it impossible. A good set-up anticipates the hand and arm swing. Indeed, it is dictated by the intention to swing the hands and arms.

Always remember this when you are "setting-up" for a shot.

Firstly, then, the set-up must be one which frees the hands and arms for the swing.

Essentially, the golf set-up is a fluid one. There is absolutely no tension or rigidity and the legs, especially, are flexed and supple. There is no room in the golf set-up for a stiff legged stance. It should be avoided at all costs.

1

2

3

The
Basic
Stance
Foundation of
the Swing

The swing of the hands and arms depends entirely upon a correct basic posture

1

CORRECT BASIC POSITION.
KEY TO SUCCESS

1.
Stand normally, chest out, with the width between the feet equal to that of the shoulders.

2.
Bend the body *forward from the waist.* This means that the back will be reasonably straight . . . definitely not hunched or curved. I STRESS THAT YOU MUST BEND FORWARD FROM THE WAIST, as if you were going to bow to somebody. As you do so, allow the knees to flex as in the illustration.

3.
If you have difficulty in achieving this bend forward from the waist, take a club, and with one hand at each end, place the shaft horizontally across the top of your legs. Now bend forward, exerting *backward pressure* on the club so that your seat is pushed back and out. This ensures a correct forward bend from the waist. Now stand erect again and assume the correct body position. Repeat often.

4.
From the correct bending forward position, place the hands and arms in position as if you were holding a club. Note that the upper arms are NOT RESTING ON THE CHEST. Quite the contrary, they are held clear of the body so that they can swing freely, *independent of the body.*

Note again that the *rump protrudes* at the rear. This must happen if you bend forward correctly *from the waist line.*

The knees, of course, are flexed. *This is vital.*

5. The Exercise
Once having perfected the bending forward posture, place the arms in the position they would be in when holding a club . . . but with the palms about a foot apart as in the illustration. Now, practice swinging the arms upward to about head height, and down again . . . *without altering the attitude of your body.*

You must not allow your body to *rise up* as you swing the arms up. This is vital. By doing this exercise we feel, perhaps for the first time, that the arms can *swing freely* from the shoulder joints, quite *independent of the body.*

Indeed, if you allow the body to rise up as the hands and arms swing up, you actually *diminish* the capacity of the hands and arms to swing. Can you feel that?

This is a vital lesson that you must learn . . . to swing the hands and arms while the body remains in position. Because as you swing the club up into the backswing the body must be trained to *maintain its height* as the club swings back and up. If you "go with" the club as it swings back you will surely destroy the swing. In fact, going with the club is "body propulsion" . . . exactly what I warned you against!

Get your position right, and repeat this exercise often. It is your first experience of "freeing off" the hands and arms from the body.

Correct basic stance.
✓ Checklist

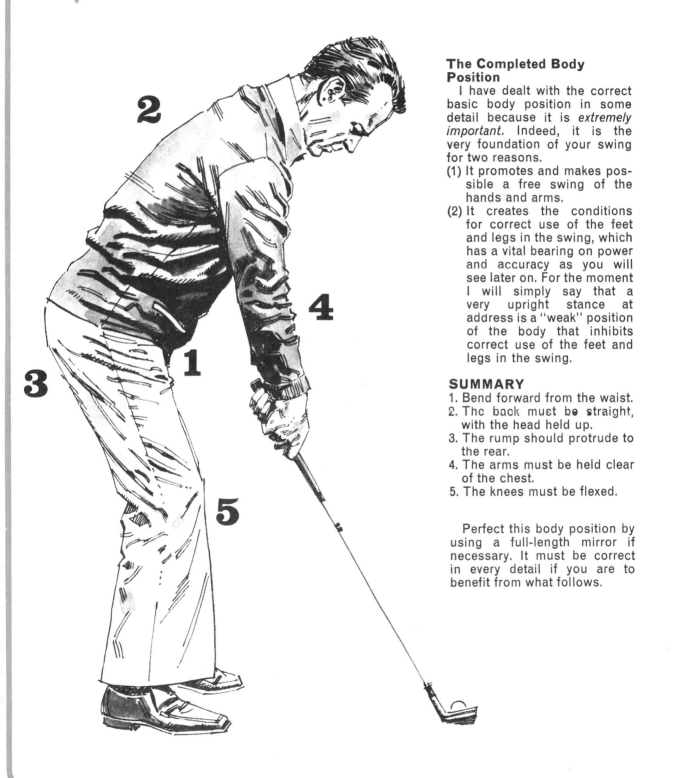

The Completed Body Position

I have dealt with the correct basic body position in some detail because it is *extremely important.* Indeed, it is the very foundation of your swing for two reasons.

(1) It promotes and makes possible a free swing of the hands and arms.

(2) It creates the conditions for correct use of the feet and legs in the swing, which has a vital bearing on power and accuracy as you will see later on. For the moment I will simply say that a very upright stance at address is a "weak" position of the body that inhibits correct use of the feet and legs in the swing.

SUMMARY

1. Bend forward from the waist.
2. The back must be straight, with the head held up.
3. The rump should protrude to the rear.
4. The arms must be held clear of the chest.
5. The knees must be flexed.

Perfect this body position by using a full-length mirror if necessary. It must be correct in every detail if you are to benefit from what follows.

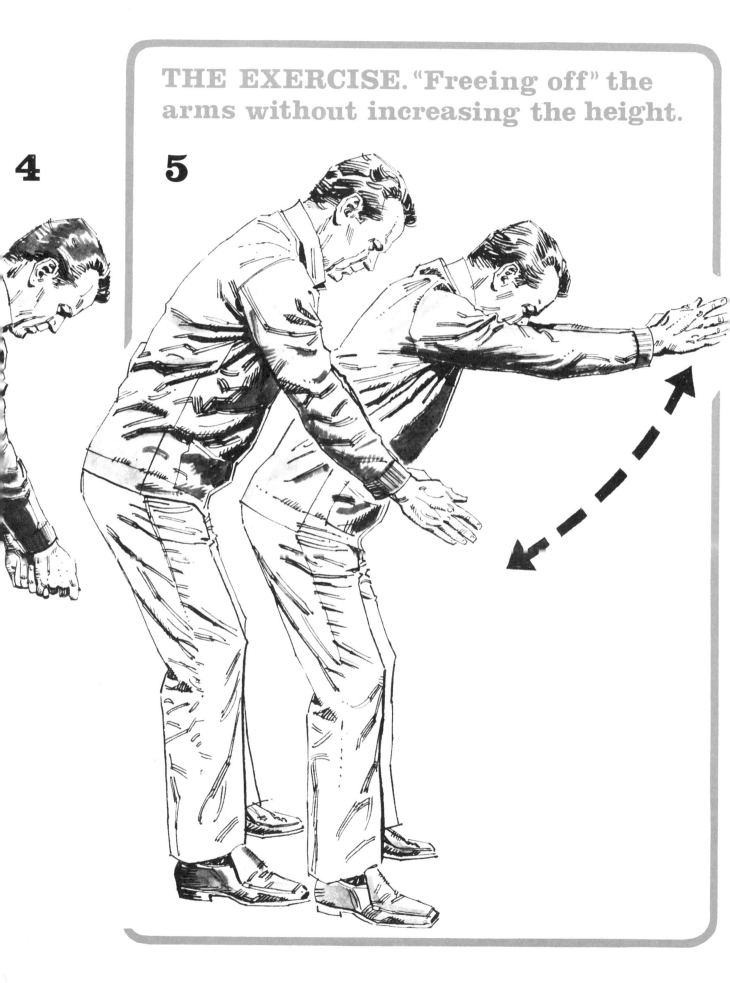

THE EXERCISE. "Freeing off" the arms without increasing the height.

4

5

Three common errors in the basic position...

I have learned by experience that many players have great difficulty in achieving a correct basic position. Here are the three most common errors.

1. A basically good position ruined by a contorted set-up of the arms. Golfers have for many years been told to place the arms in this way, with the right arm "inside" the left like this. It is very bad advice as it causes excessive elevation of the left shoulder, alters the grip and, perhaps worst of all, stiffens both arms to the point that it is impossible to swing them freely. A "body action" type swing is now required to set the hands and arms in motion.

2. The knees are correctly flexed, but this player has failed to bend forward correctly from the waist. Consequently he must round his back to get down to the ball. Note that his upper arms are in close contact with his chest! A free swing is clearly impossible from this set-up, yet it is to be seen on any golf course or range.

3. A static position. Rigid legs. No forward bend. Arms on the chest. Shoulders hunched over. This player has absolutely no idea of what he is trying to do in the golf swing. He *must* move the club by body action from a posture like this as his arms are simply not free to swing. Equally, his swing will lack power because of the rigidity of his legs. A posture like this prohibits any possibiity of correct leg movement in either back or through swing. It is a hopeless position that will breed countless errors in the swing.

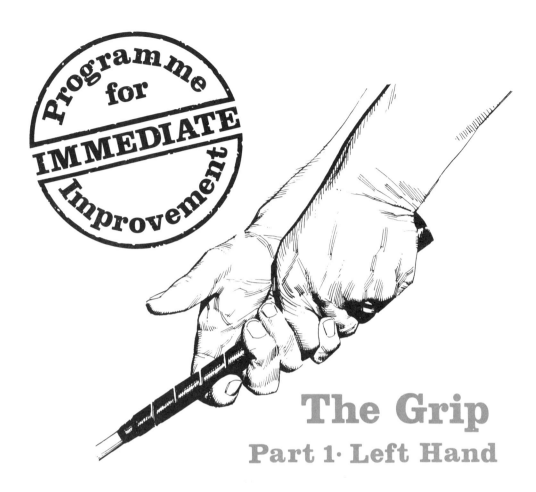

The Grip
Part 1· Left Hand

Perhaps the oldest cliche in golf instruction is that a sound grip is the foundation of a sound swing. Every golf book ever written contains a chapter about the grip, with every detail of the grip lavishly illustrated. Unfortunately, the function of the grip in the swing is less frequently discussed. If it were, players would have a better understanding of the importance of an "orthodox" grip, and how to achieve it.

As the details of the orthodox grip are so well known, how is it that so few golfers actually possess such a grip? The tragic fact is that the orthodox golf grip simply will not work for most players . . . they have too many errors in their swing actions to live with it! Most of them spend years searching for a grip . . . any grip . . . that will minimise the errors in their swings. Hence the endless variety of grotesque grips one sees on the course.

Go to any golf range. Most of the

victims can be seen fiddling with their grips, experimenting endlessly in the hope that natural selection will provide them with a position that will reduce, or eliminate the slice. They should, of course, be rebuilding their swings, not their grips!

So get your grip right, and stick to it. If you can't play golf with an orthodox grip, it's your swing that needs attention . . . not your grip. You can't cure a bad swing with an equally bad grip.

It is not generally appreciated that the set-up and grip are closely inter related. A poor set-up makes a good grip more difficult, and a bad grip affects the set-up. This is important. So relate what is said about the grip to what I say elsewhere about the set-up, particularly of the arms. They are the two sides of the same coin.

Like every other aspect of the swing, common sense principles govern the "orthodox" golf grip.

You should be aware of them.

First, what is the role of the grip in the swing? In all "bat and ball" sports we aim to get the striking surface of the "bat" (or racquet, club, etc.) moving squarely along the intended line of flight of the ball. If the face of the striking implement is not moving squarely along the intended line of flight, sidespin is imparted to the ball, and it does not fly straight.

A correct grip simply enables one to swing the club backwards (to the top), and return it to the ball (in the downswing) so that the clubface is both *square* to the intended line of flight (as it was at address), and travelling *along* the intended line of flight at impact, and slightly beyond.

A so called "good grip" will, barring other complications in the swing, bring about these two requirements. "Bad grips" make the attainment of these two conditions almost impossible.

The Left Hand.
General Principles

Left hand Grip

1. With the club correctly soled in front of you, align the open left palm to the shaft so that the *back* of the left hand squarely faces the target.

2. Close the left hand on the shaft. The thumb will be on *top* of the shaft at this stage, vertically aligned with the centre of the shaft.

3. We now turn the entire left hand slightly to the right as illustrated, so that the left thumb moves to the right side of the shaft . . . just a little. We have turned the left hand in this way simply to establish muscular contact between the fingers and wrist of the hand . . . and the left forearm. That is all. This adjustment "firms up" the entire hand and wrist. You can feel this quite distinctly. The left hand and arm can now act as a single unit, swinging the club with control. The thumb on top of the shaft (position 2) is a "weak" position of the hand in which the wrist has too much freedom to hinge. This makes control of the club-face much more difficult.

1

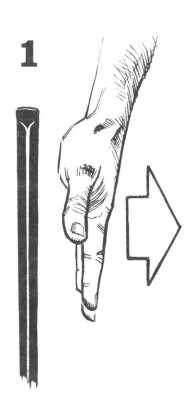

2

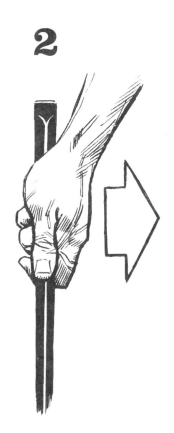

3

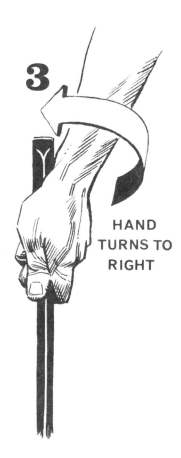

HAND TURNS TO RIGHT

Angle of the shaft

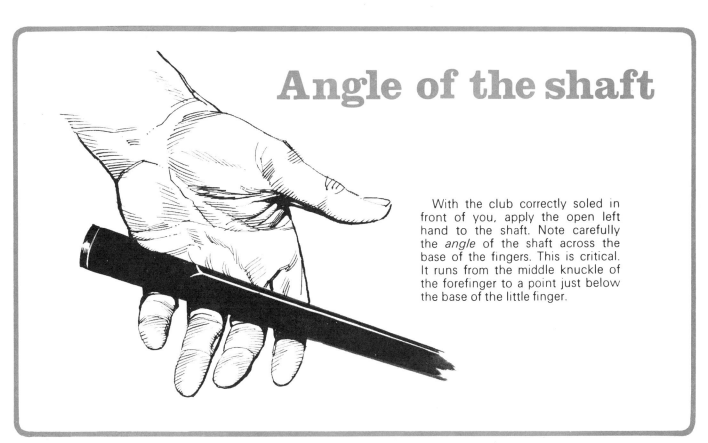

With the club correctly soled in front of you, apply the open left hand to the shaft. Note carefully the *angle* of the shaft across the base of the fingers. This is critical. It runs from the middle knuckle of the forefinger to a point just below the base of the little finger.

Spacing of fingers

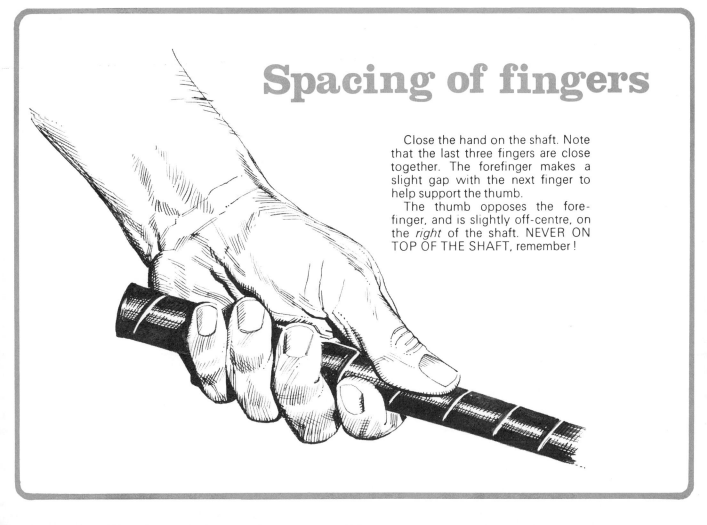

Close the hand on the shaft. Note that the last three fingers are close together. The forefinger makes a slight gap with the next finger to help support the thumb.

The thumb opposes the forefinger, and is slightly off-centre, on the *right* of the shaft. NEVER ON TOP OF THE SHAFT, remember!

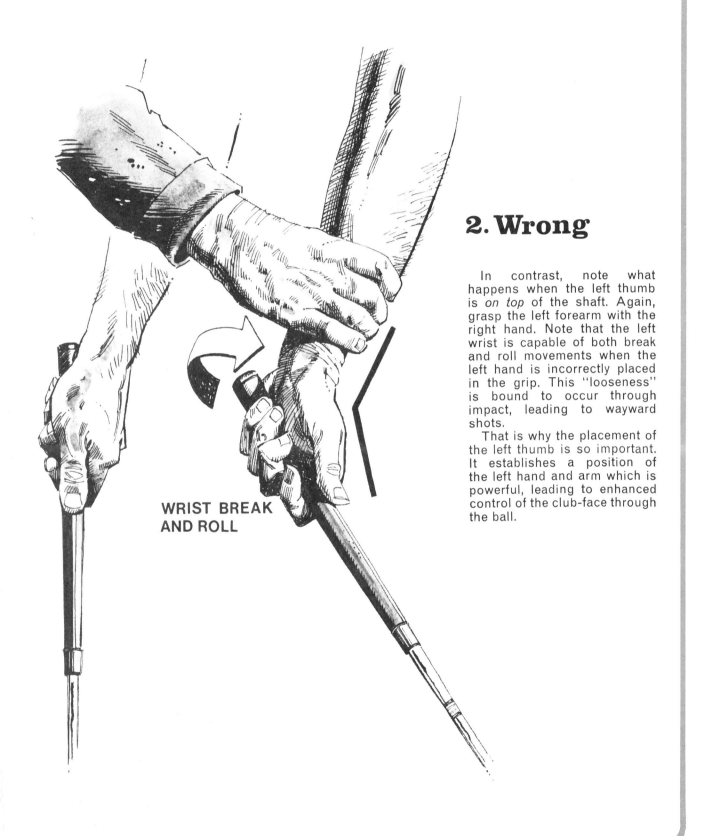

**WRIST BREAK
AND ROLL**

2. Wrong

In contrast, note what happens when the left thumb is *on top* of the shaft. Again, grasp the left forearm with the right hand. Note that the left wrist is capable of both break and roll movements when the left hand is incorrectly placed in the grip. This "looseness" is bound to occur through impact, leading to wayward shots.

That is why the placement of the left thumb is so important. It establishes a position of the left hand and arm which is powerful, leading to enhanced control of the club-face through the ball.

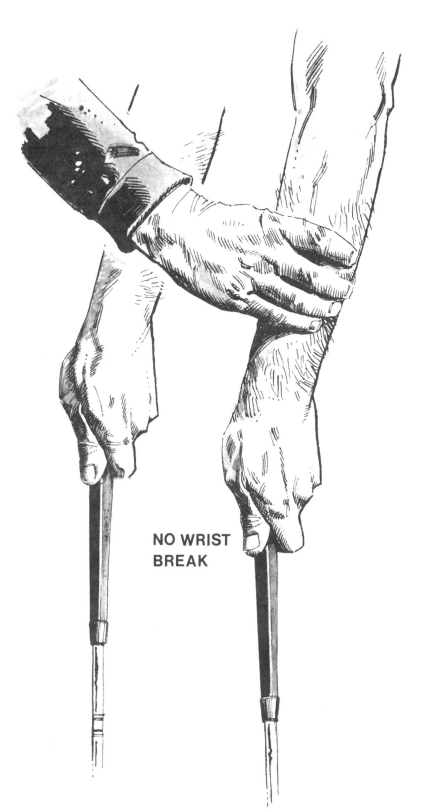

NO WRIST BREAK

1. Correct

The position of the *left thumb* on the shaft is critical. I have said that it should favour the *right* side of the shaft (picture 1), and is placed in this position by rotating the hand as described earlier.

The purpose of this adjustment was to establish muscular unity between the fingers, wrist and forearm, welding all together into a firm, controllable unit. The left arm and hand can now swing through the ball with firmness and authority, holding the face of the club square through the ball.

To test this for yourself, place the left hand correctly on the shaft as described, and grasp the left forearm with the right hand. Note that when the arm and hand is correctly placed on the shaft the possibility of independent wrist movement (breaking or rolling of the wrist through the ball) is eliminated. The hand and arm is firm, and will remain so through the stroke.

Further, by placing the left hand (and especially the thumb) correctly on the shaft, one establishes the correct left arm position (see the "arm-set") that we require in the set-up.

Firmness test

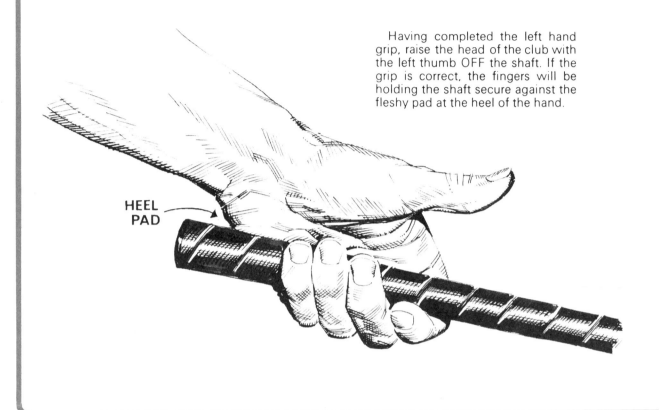

Having completed the left hand grip, raise the head of the club with the left thumb OFF the shaft. If the grip is correct, the fingers will be holding the shaft secure against the fleshy pad at the heel of the hand.

HEEL PAD

The left hand is the key to club-face control in the swing. Be sure it is correctly applied to the shaft.

The Grip
Part 2. Right Hand

As a general guide to the placement of the right hand on the grip, consider how you would place the right hand if you were going to strike something with the palm of that hand. Quite simply, you would strike the object with the palm vertical, thumb uppermost, as illustrated.

You would not place the hand in either of the positions shown in the smaller drawings, would you? The blow would lack power . . . and you would probably hurt your hand in the process. Hence grips in which the right hand is either *on top* of, or *under* the shaft have no logical basis whatsoever! Thus, the right hand is placed on the shaft so that the palm *squarely faces the target.* This is the sole guiding principle for the placement of the right hand in the grip.

Wrong basic hand positions

17

The right palm and the blade are aligned

Both squarely face the target

By placing the right hand in the grip with the palm *facing* the target, we immediately establish the idea that the right palm and the face of the club are *aligned* at all times. This is a useful concept to bear in mind as, we now know that the position of the right hand anywhere in the swing sequence will be *reflected* by the angle and position of the blade.

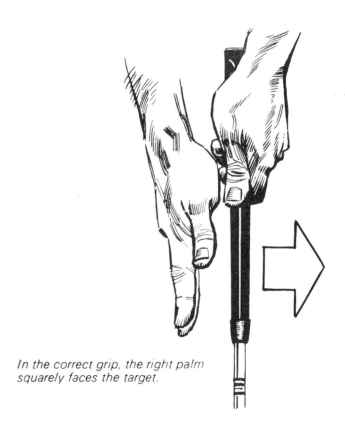

In the correct grip, the right palm squarely faces the target.

Unifying the hands to complete the grip...

Place the open palm of the right hand alongside the shaft. The palm is thus aligned with the face of the club . . . that is, they are both "looking" directly at the target. That is how they must stay. Close the two middle fingers round the shaft, with the upper of these two fingers drawn closely against the forefinger of the left hand. Now loop the right little-finger over the left forefinger, so that it rests in the space between the first two fingers of the left hand. This placement of the fingers establishes a close unity of the two hands, and is known as the Vardon overlapping grip. It has been employed by most of the world's great players, and has stood the test of time. I thoroughly recommend it to you.

Now to the right thumb and forefinger. The bent right forefinger fits snugly under the shaft, slightly separated from the other fingers. The placing of the right thumb is vital. It is *never* pressed on the top of the shaft, or still worse, on the right side of the shaft. It should lie *diagonally* across the shaft with its tip close to, or touching the tip of the right forefinger.

The grip, especially of the right hand, is mainly in the fingers. No ham-fisted palm grips please!

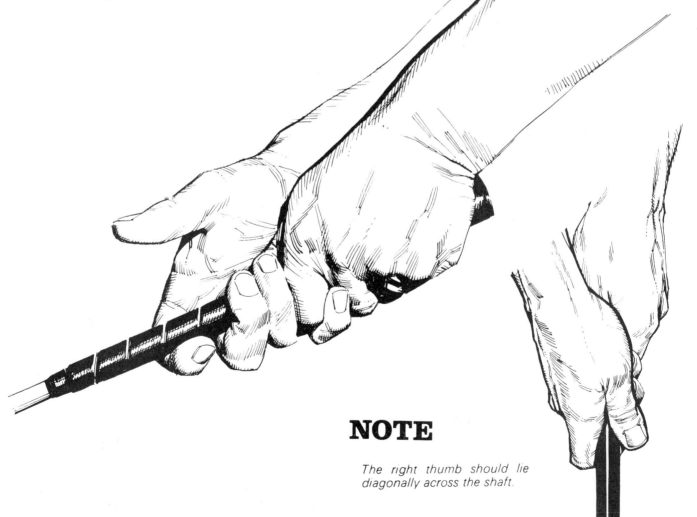

NOTE

The right thumb should lie diagonally across the shaft.

Pressure points of the GRIP

The pressure points of the grip are with the last three fingers of the left hand, and the two middle fingers of the right hand. In other words, there is absolutely no pressure between the thumbs and index fingers of either hand. If there is, the wrists and forearms are stiffened, and the swing becomes inhibited.

Remember, we grip the club to *swing* it. We cannot swing anything effectively with a fierce grip. Golf is not a game of force, so don't grip the club as if it were an axe. A sensitive, yet firm finger grip is what is required. No more . . . no less.

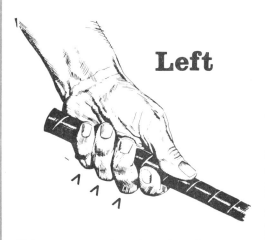

Left

Grip pressure points. Last three fingers of the left hand. Middle two fingers of the right hand. No great pressure between the thumb and index finger of either hand

Right

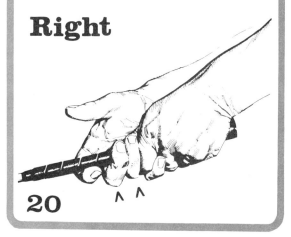

20

Finally, I repeat again. Acquire a correct grip . . . *and stick to it*, no matter what. If your grip is correct, and your shots are still going off line you must look to your swing to discover the error. You simply cannot cure a bad swing by making remedial alterations to a correct grip. In doing so you are simply compounding error! *Get your grip right, and then leave it alone.*

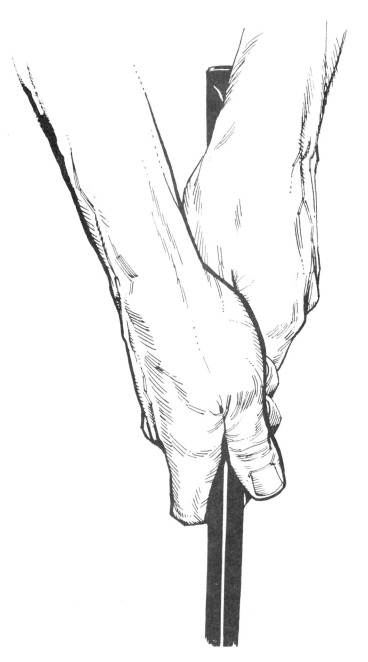

The three requirements of a sound golf swing

The golf swing MUST ACHIEVE three vital conditions in order to be effective. Few golfers are aware of them, and even fewer actually achieve them . . . and I do not exclude pros. from that category! The swing movement that I am about to describe in Lessons 2 and 3 is designed to AUTO-MATICALLY produce these three requirements. A GOOD SET-UP AND ADDRESS IS ESSENTIAL FOR THIS PURPOSE.

1 Line at impact

THE CLUB-HEAD MUST BE TRAVELLING ALONG THE INTENDED LINE OF FLIGHT THROUGH THE IMPACT AREA. Only a correct left hand and arm swing COUPLED WITH a correct body movement can achieve this line down into the ball. THE DOWNWARD SWING OF THE LEFT HAND AND ARM CREATES THE CORRECT LINE DOWN INTO, AND THROUGH THE BALL. There is no other way of doing it. Most golfers MISUSE the body in the swing, thus destroying club-line into the ball. If the club-head is not swinging "on line" you cannot hope to consistently hit straight shots.

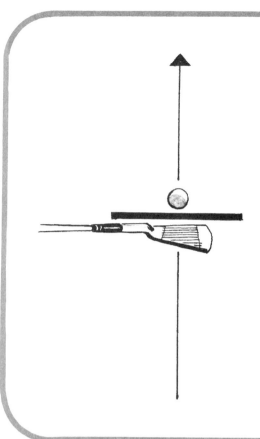

2 Square impact

The club-head must swing "on-line", but it must also be "square" to the intended line of flight through impact... AND BEYOND! To be specific, THE LEADING EDGE of the club (iron or wood) must be SQUARE (at right angles) to the intended line of flight through impact. This is largely achieved by a correct grip, and a correct hand action throughout the swing. A correct body movement also contributes to a square impact ... just as an incorrect one destroys squareness.

3 Off the middle

THE BALL MUST BE STRUCK IN THE MIDDLE OF THE CLUB-FACE WITH BOTH IRONS AND WOODS. An "on-line", square impact OFF THE MIDDLE OF THE FACE is what we must achieve ... and it is by no means common. I have seen many a tournament pro. who is incapable of hitting three consecutive balls off the middle of the face!

Hitting off the heel and toe is a sure sign of an incorrect line through impact. Actually, hitting off the toe is far more serious a fault than hitting off the "shank", as the club-line is much more "out to in" with toed shots than with shots off the "pipe". Thus, a correct swing leads to a correct club-line. Correct grip and hand action create a square impact. Given both of these, the ball will come off the middle of the face.

The address position

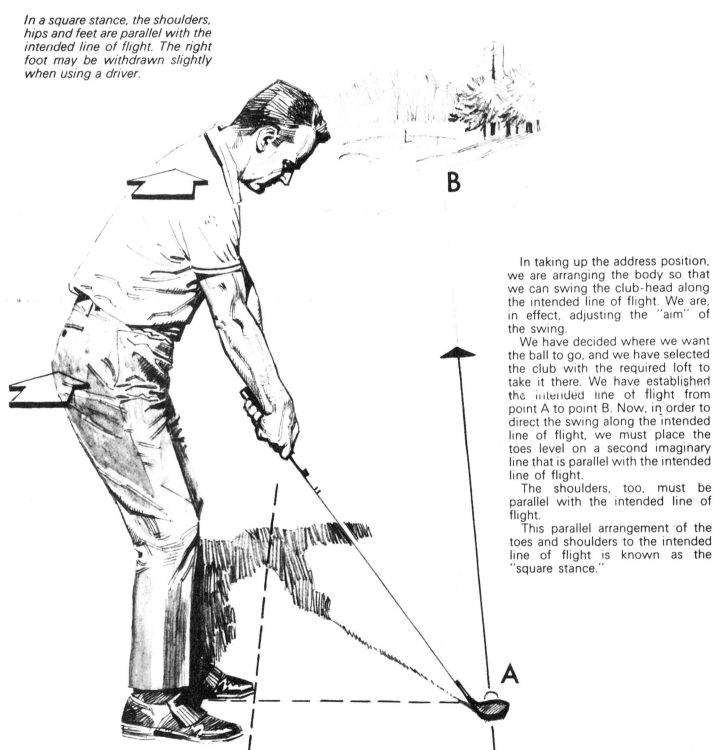

In a square stance, the shoulders, hips and feet are parallel with the intended line of flight. The right foot may be withdrawn slightly when using a driver.

B

In taking up the address position, we are arranging the body so that we can swing the club-head along the intended line of flight. We are, in effect, adjusting the "aim" of the swing.

We have decided where we want the ball to go, and we have selected the club with the required loft to take it there. We have established the intended line of flight from point A to point B. Now, in order to direct the swing along the intended line of flight, we must place the toes level on a second imaginary line that is parallel with the intended line of flight.

The shoulders, too, must be parallel with the intended line of flight.

This parallel arrangement of the toes and shoulders to the intended line of flight is known as the "square stance."

A

If the right foot alone is drawn slightly back from the line, the stance is said to be "closed."

If the left foot alone is drawn slightly back from the line, the stance to said to be "open."

For the vast majority of shots, I recommend a strictly square stance. If you want to withdraw the right foot slightly when using a driver, do so. But be sure that your shoulders and hips remain parallel to the intended line of flight. A closed stance encourages rolling of the hands through the impact area—which is why most handicappers cannot use a driver. They literally smother the shot.

I will not quarrel with a slightly open stance. But I said slightly—and again, the shoulders must be square !

I strongly recommend you not to experiment with open and closed stances. We want to swing along the intended line of flight, so let's stand square to it. Moving the feet and shoulders about merely alters the direction of the swing, and leads to complications. We are looking for a standardised procedure, remember, so let's adopt a square stance.

So the address position is mainly a matter of aligning the direction of the swing to the target—"aiming" correctly. It goes without saying that unless we align correctly at address, the ball will not go where we intend it to go. Few golfers take enough time over this vital alignment, and others think they are correctly aligned when they are not.

When practising, do not shrink from placing a club down on the ground beyond the ball, so that is parallel with the intended line of flight. By using this datum line, you can be sure that you are lining up correctly.

Visit any golf range and you will see golfers who have not even selected a specific target to aim at—so the matter of alignment never arises ! This is a sheer waste of time and effort. Always aim at a specific target, and be sure to align correctly to it. This is basic common sense. The questions of direction and distance must be resolved before we settle down to make the stroke. Uncertainty leads to tension and error.

In a closed stance, the right foot is withdrawn slightly from the line, but the hips and shoulders should remain parallel with the intended line of flight.

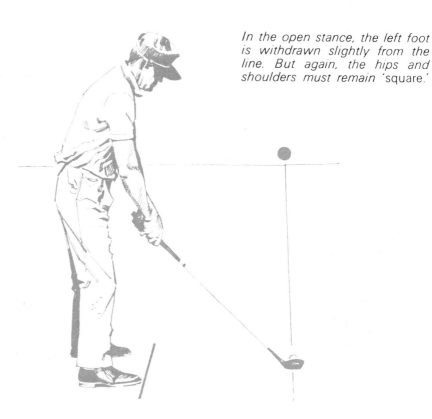

In the open stance, the left foot is withdrawn slightly from the line. But again, the hips and shoulders must remain 'square.'

Programme
for
IMMEDIATE
Improvement

Standing
to the Ball

Aligning the club-face to the hands

The arm set is established

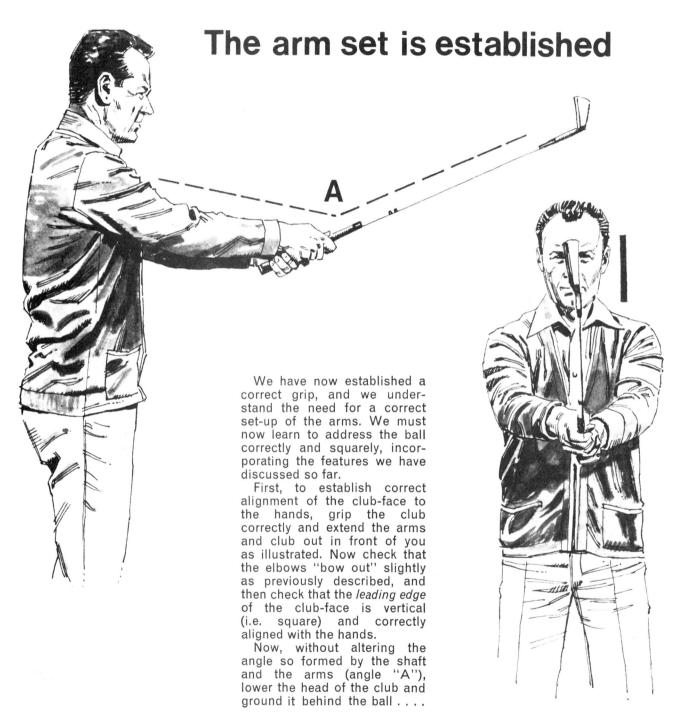

We have now established a correct grip, and we understand the need for a correct set-up of the arms. We must now learn to address the ball correctly and squarely, incorporating the features we have discussed so far.

First, to establish correct alignment of the club-face to the hands, grip the club correctly and extend the arms and club out in front of you as illustrated. Now check that the elbows "bow out" slightly as previously described, and then check that the *leading edge* of the club-face is vertical (i.e. square) and correctly aligned with the hands.

Now, without altering the angle so formed by the shaft and the arms (angle "A"), lower the head of the club and ground it behind the ball . . . .

angle 'A'
preserved

Grounding
the club

While you are lowering the head of the club you will, of course, bend forward from the waist and flex the knees. This places the club head roughly equidistant between the foot . . . and the club-head, club shaft, hands and head align down the centre of the body. In this way exaggeration at address is avoided.

This method of aligning the face of the club to the hands, and of grounding the club correctly should become a routine. It enables us to retain all the features of the set-up that we have considered previously. It also serves another useful purpose . . . opposite.

This simple drill will automatically ensure a correct position at address, free from stiffness, contortion or exaggeration of any kind.

How far from the ball at address? A drill

Many players have difficulty deciding how far from the ball they should stand at address. Naturally, with the woods you will be further from the ball than you are with the short irons, but for all types of shots, I recommend a drill which will both place you at the correct distance from the ball, and automatically place the shaft at the correct angle to the ground.

Take up your grip, and square the club-face to it. Now extend the arms and the club straight out in front of you. Avoid any forcing or stiffening of the arms, Remember, the elbows should "bow out" slightly at address. Now, maintaining the angle thus formed between the shaft and the arms, ground the club behind the ball and move the feet into position.

Both distance from the ball and shaft angle are now correct—and this drill holds good for all clubs.

In establishing the correct shaft angle, we also resolve the question of the correct position of the hands at address. Far too many players hold their hands too low at address —few hold them too high. Holding the hands too low is, as we shall see, a major cause of excessive wrist action in the swing. A vice to be avoided at all costs!

Build this routine into your address procedure, and you kill three birds with one stone!

As the head of the club is lowered, the body bends forward from the waist.

Address procedure

First, stand behind the ball looking in the direction of the intended shot, and establish an imaginary line to the target. At the same time, pick out a distinct landmark or object (bush, tree, post, church spire, etc.) directly beyond the target area to serve as a specific aiming point.

You have already chosen a club to give you the required distance for the shot you intend to play. You now have a specific object at which to aim. Thus, direction and distance have been resolved, and you can now concentrate solely on the stroke.

While this process of evaluating the shot has been going on, the good player will have been subconsciously forming his grip on the club, and "feeling" the stroke in his hands. He will check that the club-face is "squared" to his grip, and then he will approach the ball and ground the club behind it.

In grounding the club, he will ensure that the face of the club is square (at right angles) to the intended line of flight.

He will then position his feet with frequent reference to the aiming point that he has previously selected. Having placed the feet, he is ready to play his shot.

Note that the positioning of the feet came LAST.

The average golfer often reverses this procedure, placing his feet first, then vaguely grounding the club he juggles with his grip in an attempt to get the club-face square.

There is no logical sequence in his method, and his last minute grip adjustments account for the fact that his grip is never the same from one shot to the next.

We have already said that golf is a game of consistency. So let's be consistent, and develop correct routines for everything. Good golf is largely a matter of forming good habits. Here, once again, is the routine. (1) Evaluate the shot. (2) Take up your grip and square the club-face to it. (3) Ground the club correctly behind the ball. (4) Now place the feet in position.

The arms should bow out slightly at address

The grip, and the set-up of the arms are verly closely related. A poor arm set-up makes a good grip more difficult, and a bad grip affects the arm set-up. This is not generally realised.

Contortions of the arms at address are common among golfers, resulting, I fear, from bad advice. Contorted arms are stiff arms, and you cannot freely swing a rigid limb.

I have told you to hold the arms clear of the body. Now, to achieve a correct arm set-up, simply bring the hands together in front of you, palms facing each other (you do not need a club for this), and close the hands as if you were placing them on a club—right hand below the left. Now look at your arms. The first thing you will notice (if they are relaxed) is that the arms "bow" out slightly at the elbows. This is exactly the set-up we want. Check it in front of a mirror.

There is no straightening or stiffening of the arms whatsoever. Neither is there any twisting inwards of the elbows to bring them close together, as has been advised by some eminent players who do not themselves set the arms that way.

The set-up I require is quite easy to achieve. Don't complicate it needlessly.

It is very important that you achieve the arm set-up that I have described. It will save you a lot of heartache later on, as a poor arm set-up profoundly affects your play.

I have started by correcting the arm set-up of many a top player, which has automatically resolved other problems at the top of the swing.

I cannot overstress the importance of a good arm set-up.

Do not twist the elbows inwards to bring them close together.

right

wrong

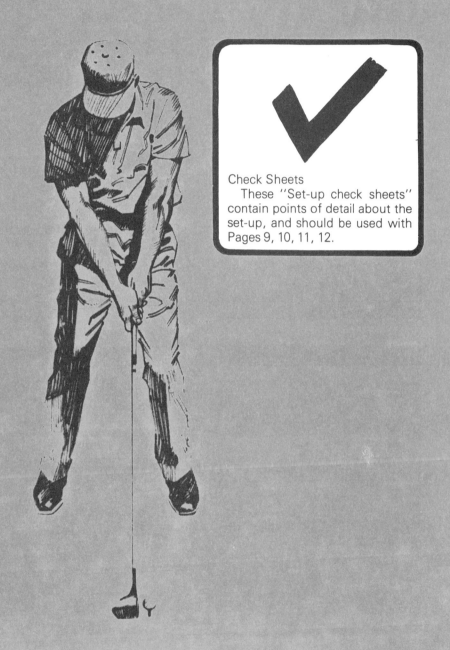

Check Sheets

These "Set-up check sheets" contain points of detail about the set-up, and should be used with Pages 9, 10, 11, 12.

Set up check sheet·1

1

Weight

The weight is taken evenly between the feet, favouring neither right or left foot. Likewise, the weight is supported by the whole of the underside of the foot, it is neither thrown forward on to the ball of the foot, or backwards on the heel. The feet remain active throughout the entire swing action. Indeed, it is the feet that motivate the swing. They must never be "planted down" as if you are trying to put down roots. They must be "live," ready to create movement.

2

Flexed knees

The knees are flexed. This is vitally important. Think of a tennis player waiting on the base line to receive a serve. He is alert and active, and his body is poised and relaxed . . . ready for action. His legs are live and fluid. Likewise a boxer. The legs are flexed and mobile. There is no room in the golf set-up for a stiff legged stance. Stiff legs are inactive legs.

The flexing of the right leg, particularly, is important. Indeed, it is flexed in the set-up, and it will remain flexed throughout the entire backswing movement. There is absolutely no straightening of the right leg during the backswing. I will deal with this point more fully in the next lesson . . . but you should be aware in taking up your stance that the flexed position of the right leg will remain unchanged throughout the backswing. Remember that.

3

Inward flexing

The right knee should be inclined slightly inwards. Inward flexing means that this knee is turned in slightly towards the ball, with the consequence that the weight which the right foot has to bear will be mainly on the *inside* of that foot. Why is the right knee flexed inwards? Because, in the backswing, the body turn takes place on the "platform" set up by the right knee, above which the right hip is cleared to the rear. The flexed right leg in fact supports the swing like a buttress, guarding against a sway to the right, and ensuring that a genuine turn takes place in the backswing, rather than a rocking motion. This is just a word of explanation. Do not concern yourself too much with the backswing just yet. I am simply trying to suggest why inward flexing of the right knee is desirable in the set-up.

The body bends forward from the waist, with the back straight. We don't lean forward . . . or stoop . . . and the head is held up. Some players have a lot of difficulty in arriving at a correct position here, so look closely at the drawing and be guided by it. Note that the spine is not curved and the shoulders are not hunched.

Really, the best guide in taking up this position is simply to remember that we are taking up a position to swing the hands and arms. If you bear this in mind, exaggeration will be avoided.

Posture 4

33

Ball placement
Avoiding extremes

We have established the intended line of flight to the target, and we are going to place the toes level on a second imaginary line that is parallel with the intended line of flight.

But where should the ball be in relation to the feet in the stance?

Starting with the drive, the ball should be played from a point opposite the inside of the left heel. That is as far to the left as the ball should ever go in the stance.

As we move down through the bag, fairway woods, long irons, medium irons, to the short irons, the ball moves progressively to the right in the stance— until it reaches the halfway point between the feet, and there it stops.

Never play the ball on the right side of the halfway line. If you do, the set-up (particularly of the arms) which you have so carefully cultivated is distorted and out of position, and error is bound to result.

Centre, or forward of centre.

BALL PLACEMENT

short irons

fairway woods & long irons

DRIVER

SHORT IRON

The ball moves from the inside of the left heel, back to the halfway point as we go through the bag from long to short clubs. Never further back than halfway.

Check Sheets
These "Set-up check sheets" contain points of detail about the set-up.

Set up check sheet·2

5 Left shoulder

The right shoulder is slightly lower than the left. I said "slightly." After all, the right hand is lower than the left on the shaft. I warn you against elevating the left shoulder excessively. It cramps and distorts the set-up, and what is worse, blocks a free swing of the left hand and arm. It is a stiff, rigid position, and one which, over the years, I have come to recognise as a symptom of a body-heaver rather than a swinger. It is the hallmark of the golfer who propels the arms to the top of the swing with a turn of the body . . . rather than swinging the arms to the top and allowing the body to respond to the swing.

Please avoid it. It is so often seen, and yet is very harmful.

6

Above all, get those arms *clear* of the chest. Move them out so that you can feel space under the arms. You simply cannot swing the arms if the upper arm is in contact with the chest. If you start with the arms in contact with the chest, you will have to turn the body to get the arms moving. This is the root of all evil in the swing! So get those arms clear of the chest and sense the swinging motion that is about to begin. Get the feeling that, as your hands and arms begin to swing back, your shoulders will respond to this movement by turning, in order that the swing may develop further.

This set-up takes the effort out of the backswing. From here, we can swing the hands and arms up into the backswing in a free, effortless movement. We can sense the power that can be generated by this type of free swing.

As a player learns to swing his hands and arms, he will notice that his grip on the shaft becomes much lighter. This is a sure sign that he is relying more on "swing" and less on "muscle" for club-head speed.

Arms

Head 7

The head is central, and inclined very slightly to the right. Both eyes are looking at the ball. Again, exaggerated positions of the head are so often seen in the set-up . . . often as the result of advice from top international golfers! Players are advised to incline the head well to the right, or turn the head to the right, sighting the ball with the left eye only . . . and so on. Avoid such advice. These mannerisms are all very well for top players who have full control of their swing actions, but for the average player, they invariably lead to error.

The head is, after all, an extremely heavy item of the anatomy. If its weight is thrown to one side, it can seriously affect the symmetry and balance of the swing. Further, placing it to the right (well behind the ball) often results in it being shifted to the left in the course of the downswing, with disastrous results. No, do not experiment with head positions. It can lead to serious errors in the takeaway and downswing. And look at the ball with both eyes. You have two eyes . . . use them!

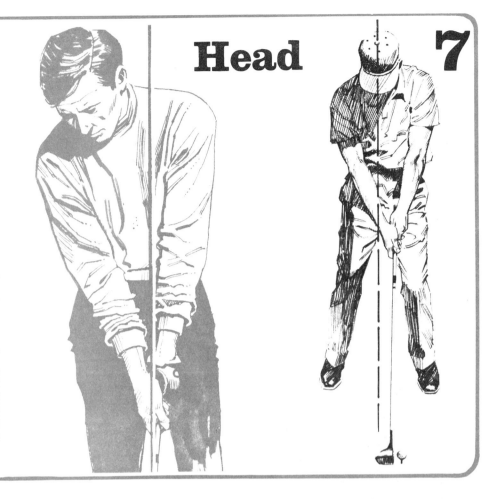

8 Hands

The hands are held "up" in the correct set-up. Most players hold their hands too low when addressing the ball. Again, study the drawing, noting the convex curve about the thumb knuckle. The wrists are slightly "arched." The reverse is often seen with the hands at a concave angle to the forearm.

With the hands held low, pronounced rolling of the wrists through the impact area is possible . . . and frequently occurs. With them held up, however, the wrists and forearms behave more as a single unit, eliminating unnecessary movement of the wrists . . . and consequently eliminating error in the position of the club-face at impact.

A great deal of inaccurate striking results from sloppy wrists through the ball, originating in a faulty position of the hands in the set-up. It can be so easily corrected, and a much firmer control of the club-face results, with improved accuracy as a bonus.

Foot placement
Ball central, or forward of centre

Generally speaking, the position of the ball for all shots should vary little. Again, we are looking for standardisation and consistency. This is impossible if the ball is shifted forward and backwards like a shuttle on a loom.

We may deviate from this rule with the wedge and approach type shots, where bunkers and other hazards have to be negotiated. But for standard shots on the fairway with all clubs, play the ball off the centre, or forward of centre—please.

The width of the stance decreases as you go down through the clubs from driver to short irons.

With the driver, the distance between the feet should be roughly equal to the width of the shoulders.

The distance decreases progressively until, with the short irons, the feet may be as little as 12 inches apart between the insides of the heels. But what I have said about ball placement still holds good.

Whatever the width, the right foot is set square to the line. That is, pointing to twelve o'clock—or straight ahead.

The left foot does not point straight ahead, but is inclined slightly towards the target—about the five to twelve position.

This is simply a natural position of the feet for the type of action that the golf swing is. If you were throwing a ball, you would place the feet in the same way.

Try it. It is simply a matter of comfort and being relaxed.

A. Driver & woods
B. Long irons
C. Medium/short irons

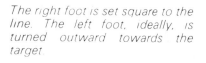

The right foot is set square to the line. The left foot, ideally, is turned outward towards the target.

The job of the golf swing

We have covered the set-up and address at some length . . . and quite rightly. These fundamentals are often overlooked by amateur and pro alike, yet they are absolutely vital to good golf. Time taken in checking your grip, set-up and address alignment is never wasted.

Now, we are nearing the first phase of the swing movement . . . the Backswing. But first, let's pause to ask a very fundamental question . . . WHAT ARE WE TRYING TO DO IN THE GOLF SWING? It is essential to answer this question CLEARLY . . . and keep that answer in mind all of the time. It is a remarkable fact that few golfers have a really clear idea of what they are trying to achieve with their swings.

The job of the golf swing…
A square impact into and along the intended line of flight

First, we are trying to propel the ball STRAIGHT from point A to point B . . . from where it lies to a selected target area. This establishes the concept of a line from the ball to the target . . . THE INTENDED LINE OF FLIGHT. Clearly, if the ball is to move along the intended line of flight, the club-face (or blade) MUST BE MOVING SQUARELY ALONG THE INTENDED LINE OF FLIGHT DURING IMPACT . . . and for as long as possible *before* and *after* impact.

This holds good for every golf stroke, from the putt to the drive.

With this central idea in mind, we can define the job of the golf swing. THE GOLF SWING IS A MOVEMENT WHICH CAUSES THE CLUB HEAD TO SWING INTO AND ALONG THE INTENDED LINE OF FLIGHT THROUGH THE IMPACT AREA AND BEYOND . . . WITH THE FACE OF THE CLUB SQUARE TO THAT LINE.

This is the guiding principle for everything that we do in building a new swing. If ever your swing "goes off" it is because these conditions are not being met. Indeed, we can say that a good swing brings about these conditions, and a bad swing does not. It is as simple as that!

Thus, we see that it is the section of the swing arc *between the feet* . . . the impact zone . . that is the key area. It is what happens here that determines the quality of the shot. This area I term THE APEX OF THE SWING.

As I said earlier, the club head must be moving squarely along the intended line of flight BEFORE THE BALL IS STRUCK . . . and REMAIN on that line well AFTER IMPACT. The longer the club-head remains on the intended line of flight through impact, the better. Or as the Americans put it, we aim to hit the ball FOR A LONG TIME!

This DRIVING FORWARD OF THE BALL is what produces the long, accurate shot that can hold its direction in wind. This is the quality of impact that compresses the golf ball on the club-face like a fried egg at the moment of impact. This is the type of impact that leads to powerful, accurate shot-making, and low scores.

I said that the impact zone of the swing was the APEX. Now I want you to think in terms of a LONG SWING APEX. That is a STRAIGHT, SUSTAINED CONTACT WITH THE BALL THROUGH IMPACT . . . ALONG THE INTENDED LINE OF FLIGHT.

That is what the golf swing is all about. That is why we stand square to the intended line of flight. That is why the swing plane must be properly aligned. That is why we must be aware of "CLUB-LINE" . . . or the direction that the club-head is taking through the ball.

Never lose sight of this vital concept of CLUB-LINE THROUGH THE BALL.

The 'long apex'... a straight, sustained contact with the ball through impact

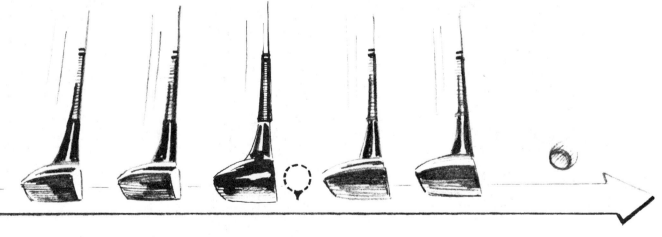

It is not enough merely
to hit the ball···the club
head __must__ swing squarely
along the intended line of flight
through impact and beyond

 Programme for IMMEDIATE Improvement

A vital Exercise

"FRONT-END THERAPY"

I am now going to introduce you to an exercise which will prepare you for the new backswing that you will learn in the next lesson.

This exercise, which I call "front-end therapy" has quickly transformed the swings (and scores) of thousands of players because it establishes early the principle that we must swing freely into and *along* the intended line of flight with a square blade . . . *driving* the ball powerfully forward. This creates both accuracy and power.

You may find it novel that we are dealing with the "front end" (the through swing) of the movement first, before correcting the

backswing. However, it is a fact that unless your movement through the ball is correct (a square impact into and *along* the intended line of flight), the best backswing in the world is of no avail at all! After all, the backswing itself is "shaped" by the intention to swing squarely *along* the intended line of flight through impact.

So we get the most important part of the movement right first. Then we add to it a correct backswing.

THE MOST COMMON PROBLEM IN GOLF

All poor players, without exception, start the downswing by

turning the shoulders *first,* while the feet remain *static.* This, of course, throws the club out of line from the top, and any possibility of a correct downswing is instantly ruined.

In fact, in a correct downswing, the body should unwind from the feet . . . up. This means that the feet and legs should come into play *first,* with the shoulders unwinding *last!* In other words, the shoulder line must *never* run ahead of the hip line in the downswing.

THIS CORRECT DOWNSWING IS ACHIEVED BY PROPER LEG ACTION IN THE SWING, and this exercise shows you how to acquire good foot and leg action...

THIS EXERCISE CAN TRANSFORM YOUR GOLF ALMOST IMMEDIATELY !

EXERCISE PRELIMINARY

First, assume the correct address position and, with a 7 iron in your hands, "free off" the arms by moving them up and down in front of you as described earlier. Remember to keep the height constant . . . *do not* allow the body to rise up as you swing the club up! The purpose of this exercise, you will remember, is to get the feeling that the hands and arms can *swing freely from the shoulders* while the body retains its position.

We are now going to apply this principle to the swing movement. . .

THE EXERCISE

1. Ground the club as if you were addressing the ball.

2. Move the club-head forward . . . along the intended line of flight . . . noting that the *right heel* immediately comes off the ground, and the right knee begins to fold in towards the left.

NOTE. Do not allow your body to rise up *or* move in the direction of the hand and arm swing!

3. As the hands and arms swing the club up to about shoulder height (note that the blade is dead square), the right heel is *well clear* of the ground and the weight has moved to the *inside* of the right foot. The right knee has moved progressively closer in toward the left knee. The player's *height* has not increased!

4, 5. As the hands and arms swing the club up into the finish, the right foot comes *up on to the toe.*

6. The finish of the stroke. The right knee is now *alongside* the left. The right foot is now balanced up *on the toe,* and the foot is *vertical.* THIS IS MOST IMPORTANT. The player now drops his hands to waist level and checks that the blade is still *square,* as it was at address.

1

SHOULDERS
MUST BE SQUARE
AT THE START

2

44

Do this exercise slowly at first, and be sure to bring the right foot and knee into play *as soon* as the exercise begins. Then, place a ball down, and, taking a short backswing of about two feet, go into the exercise again . . . this time striking the ball.

CORRECT FOOT AND LEG ACTION ENABLES THE SHOULDERS TO UNWIND LAST. THE CLUB CAN THEN SWING SQUARELY "ON LINE."

3 **4** **5** **6**

NOTICE THAT THE PLAYER'S HEIGHT REMAINS
CONSTANT··· HE DOESN'T RISE UP THROUGH THE
BALL. THIS HOLDS THE CLUB SQUARELY ON LINE,

CREATING ACCURACY AND POWER···

NOTE. Correct foot and leg action has an important bearing on power in the swing. It is too early to discuss this now, but when you reach page 125 of the third lesson, return again to "front end therapy" and read it with greater understanding.

BENEFITS OF THE EXERCISE

By doing this exercise we acquire "swing" and "club-line".

We establish again that the *hands and arms* swing the club in the golf movement. The shoulders *react* to this swing by turning after *impact* simply and solely to permit the swing to progress freely up to the finish of the stroke. In so doing, the club-head remains squarely on the line of flight for an *extended* period of time. This is what good "club-line" through the ball means.

If the shoulders are moving the club, a line through the ball cannot be achieved. The club comes abruptly off line after . . . and often *before* . . . impact, with disastrous results.

Only the hands and arms can swing on line, through the ball. Thus, the shoulders *must* be square at impact if the club is to meet the ball squarely . . . and then the shoulders *turn* to enable the hands and arms to continue to swing freely *on the line* through impact and beyond. This is what creates accuracy and power.

I say again, if the body rises up, or "goes with" the club as it swings through impact, club-line is lost and the swing of the hands and arms is totally destroyed.

Correct foot and leg action enables you to "unwind" the shoulders *last* . . . and then only to enable the hands and arms to continue swinging "on the line" clear up to the finish.

This results in a correct finish, as in illustration A. If the shoulders unwind first, the result is the posture in illustration B. Clearly, the club-head *has not* remained on line, and therefore the ball will not fly straight.

By mastering this exercise your shotmaking *must* immediately improve. Correct foot and leg action is enabling your shoulders to unwind *last,* hence, the shoulders are square at impact, creating a square contact with the ball. Then, your shoulders unwind *after impact* (never, never before!) to permit the hands and arms to continue swinging freely from the shoulders, *holding* the line as they do so.

You 'are, in fact, swinging the club *squarely* in the direction that you want the ball to go. Along the line of flight!

Misuse of the shoulders creates a circular arc through the ball which, of course, can never result in a straight shot.

So swing freely, and you will hold your "line".

Unwind with the shoulders and you will destroy "line".

And the key to it all is *correct foot and leg action*!

A
ON LINE

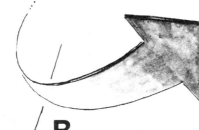

B
EARLY SHOULDER
TURN TAKES CLUB
OFF LINE

LESSON 2
The sole purpose of the backswing is to correctly position the club at the top ...

it has absolutely nothing to do with 'generating power'

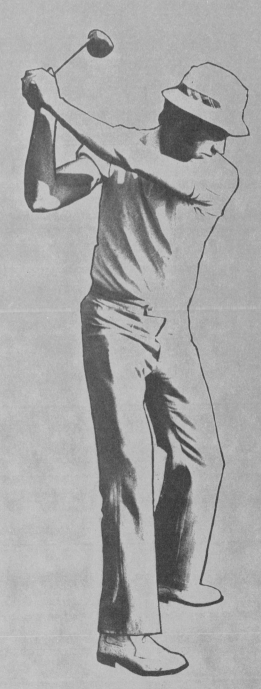

You have probably been told that the purpose of the backswing is to "generate power." Forget it! It does nothing of the kind.

The backswing is a POSITIONAL MOVEMENT. You do not hit the ball on the backswing ... that comes later! You are merely CORRECTLY POSITIONING THE CLUB AT THE TOP OF THE SWING ALIGNING IT ACCURATELY ... for the downward swing into and along the intended line of flight. If the club is out of position at the top a correct downswing will be virtually impossible without some compensatory movement.

Actually the backswing has a great deal in common with the set-up and address positions. In the set-up we *positioned* the body for a free swing of the left hand and arm. At address we adopted a square stance so that the "aim" of the swing would be right. Now again, in the backswing, we are simply *positioning* the club ... and the body ... for the downward swing into the ball ... into and along the intended line of flight.

In other words the backswing is a *precision* movement ... and like all other precision movements it is peformed at moderate speed and with an absence of force. It is vital to see the backswing as a "passive" phase of the swing movement. If you associate it with power and force you will never get the club into position at the top, and the swing will be wrecked.

Forget all you have read about the "coiled up power of the backswing" and the "resistance between the hips and shoulders in the backswing that is unleashed into the ball in the downswing," etc., etc. These concepts are sheer dynamite and stem from the myth that the backswing is for "generating power."

Think of a marksman taking aim on his target. He does it calmly and with precision. The rifle must be correctly aligned *before* he pulls the trigger. Likewise an archer. He positions his bow with precision *before* releasing the arrow. That's all we're doing in the backswing. Aligning the club correctly in preparation for the "release." If it is not correctly aligned (or aimed if you prefer), like the marksman or the archer, we are sure to be off target. It is as simple as that!

right

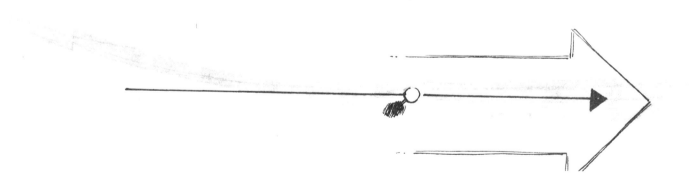

I have referred to a "correct position at the top." This requires definition, and why is it so important?
AT THE TOP OF THE BACKSWING THE SHAFT OF THE DRIVER IS ALMOST HORIZONTAL TO THE GROUND, AND PARALLEL WITH THE INTENDED LINE OF FLIGHT. The left hand and arm swings the club up into this position. The role of the body is to *create the conditions* for this full arm swing.
From this CORRECT TOP-OF-THE-SWING POSITION the left hand and arm can REVERSE DIRECTION SMOOTHLY into the downswing and achieve a blow into and along the intended line of flight.

wrong

But if the shaft does not achieve this correct position at the top and is mis-aligned . . . that is, pointing either to right or left of the target . . . a downward swing into and along the intended line of flight will be IMPOSSIBLE without compensatory movement in the downswing. Such compensatory movements are the beginnings of an unsound action. We want to keep the movement as simple as possible, with all superflous motion eliminated.

Golfers fail to achieve a correct position at the top for two main reasons. First, they do not *turn fully* in the backswing so the club can never reach the correct position and, second, they do not employ the body in the right way. They allow it to hinder rather than assist the swing. We are about to see how a *full turn* is achieved, and how the body turn is "shaped" and controlled so that it assists the swing of the left hand and arm instead of destroying that swing.

Why a full shoulder turn is necessary

Incomplete turn ··· out of position at the top

OUT-TO-IN

Many of the world's top golfers assert that "a full shoulder turn is necessary for power". I have said that the backswing has nothing to do with generating power. Its purpose is simply to correctly position the club at the top in readiness for the downward swing.

I think it is a mistake to associate the backswing with power. After all, you don't hit the ball on the backswing. That comes later. Thinking "power" tends to make the backswing quick and jerky, and this results in an incomplete turn.

Your backswing thought should NOT be about "a full shoulder turn in order to generate power". Rather, you should think in terms of a full shoulder turn TO ALLOW THE LEFT HAND AND ARM TO SWING FULLY INTO A CORRECT POSITION AT THE TOP. From there it can swing down again into the ball on a correct line through impact. This is what creates power and straightness.

The illustration shows what happens when the backswing is incomplete. The club is out of position at the top and therefore a correct downswing line (into and along the intended line of flight through impact) cannot be achieved. An out-to-in clubline is almost certain to result.

COMPLETE THE BACKSWING FIRST. DO IT SMOOTHLY AND WITH PLENTY OF TIME. Power is released at a late stage in the downswing. Don't run ahead of the correct sequence!

We now know what we want to achieve in the backswing. Now let's consider *how* it is done.

I have already stressed at length that the golf action consists mainly of a FREE SWING OF THE LEFT HAND AND ARM to the top . . . and down again into and through the ball. A correct body turn makes this swing possible. It does not *cause* the movement of the left hand and arm at any time. By turning correctly the body *creates the conditions* for full leverage of the left hand and arm. We will now see precisely why the left hand and arm is paramount in the swing. First, the swing of the left hand and arm imparts MOVEMENT to the club-head at all times in the swing. Second, the left hand and arm controls the DIRECTION (club-line) that the club-head takes in the swing. Third, the swing of the left hand and arm creates the SWING PLANE and finally, the angle of the club-face is CONTROLLED by the left hand.

Hence MOVEMENT, DIRECTION, SWING PLANE AND CONTROL are all governed by the swing of the left hand and arm! That is why I maintain that the swinging of the left hand and arm is the basis of the golf swing itself.

The swinging of the left hand and arm is the basis of the golf action

Now let's take a brief look at the complete backswing movement. Here it is in essence with the left hand and arm swinging the club to the top, and the body turning in a controlled manner to create the conditions for the full swing. Note that the swinging movement of the arm and hand *alone has created the swing plane.* The left hand, the club-shaft and the club-head have moved on the plane at all times . . . and they will remain *on the same plane* in the downswing, thus ensuring an impact into and along the intended line of flight. Remember that !

Actually, the swinging of the club with the left hand and arm *alone* is a most valuable exercise. It is literally the essence of the backswing and helps to develop "left side control" in the swing. But do it reasonably slowly and be sure to get that club-shaft positioned correctly at the top as it is here.

Above all, try to sense how a correct body turn promotes a full swing of the left hand and arm. An incorrect turn destroys the capacity of the arm to swing ! Remember, a correct body turn and a full, free swing of the left hand and arm are complimentary. We cannot have one without the other. But the BODY DOES NOT PROPEL THE ARM TO THE TOP.

By achieving a correct body movement the left hand and arm is FREED TO SWING TO THE FULLEST EXTENT AND CAN DEVELOP MAXIMUM LEVERAGE. Once you have acquired this movement your game must improve !

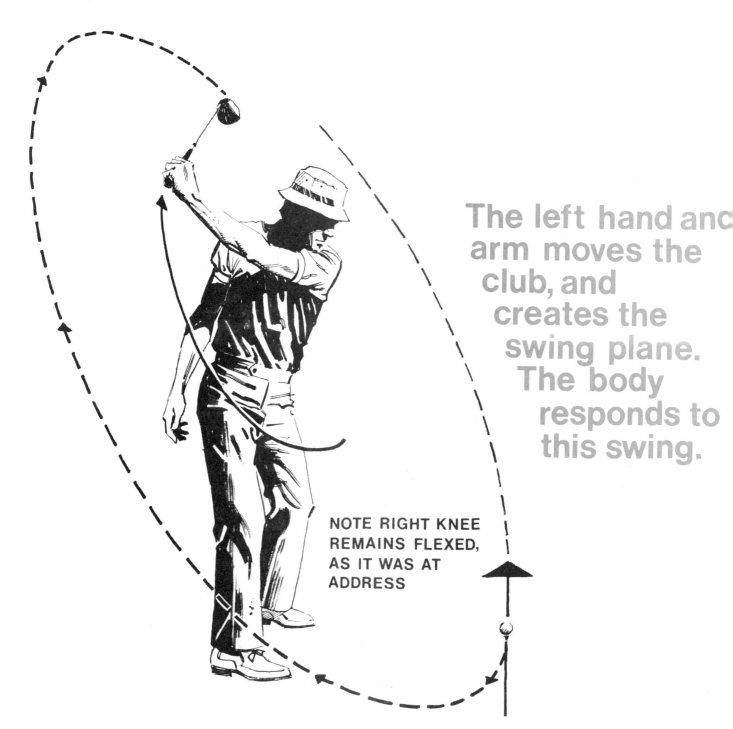

The left hand and arm moves the club, and creates the swing plane. The body responds to this swing.

NOTE RIGHT KNEE REMAINS FLEXED, AS IT WAS AT ADDRESS

Starting the swing

THE METHOD

We are correctly set-up to the ball and are ready to begin the backswing. How exactly does the swing start? The movement back from the ball is made by THE LEFT HAND AND ARM. You do not need a club in your hand to discover this. Simply assume the correct set-up position with the left hand and arm extended, thumb uppermost . . . pointing the fingertips at the ball Now, keeping the shoulders *still*, simply move the left hand and arm backwards from the ball taking care not to alter the vertical alignment of the palm (or in other words, don't roll the wrist).
THE ARC SO TRACED OUT IS THE CORRECT TAKEAWAY PATH.

Note that the correct takeaway line is not "straight back from the ball" as some teachers insist. Neither have you made any conscious effort to steer your hand into an "inside takeaway." It is a perfectly natural arc back from the ball. Do not complicate it.
THIS IS THE TAKEAWAY LINE THAT WILL TAKE THE CLUB BACK INTO THE PLANE THAT WE DESIRE. So we see that good club-line begins *the moment the club-head is set in motion.*
Any other method of starting the takeaway will produce a different takeaway line, and consequently a different swing plane . . . and if the plane of the swing is misaligned the club MUST BE OUT OF POSITION AT THE TOP.

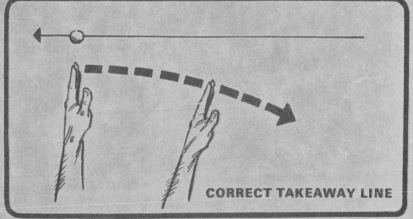

CORRECT TAKEAWAY LINE

The swing is started by a backward movement of the left hand and arm···

Now let's repeat the left hand and arm movement with a club in the hand. Keep the *shoulders still* and move the club-head back by moving the left hand and arm as described. Now, since the shoulders are square (at address) the left hand and arm can only move the club-head backwards from the ball, along the arc, for a distance of *about a foot before being blocked* by the square position of the shoulders. Try this.

IT IS AT THIS POINT IN THE BACKSWING MOVEMENT THAT THE SHOULDERS SHOULD BEGIN TO TURN . . AND NOT BEFORE! They now turn to allow the left hand and arm (and the club-head) to *continue* to swing freely back along the arc . . . all the way to the top of the swing. Thus, we see in action the principle that the body *does not propel* the arms. Quite the reverse. The hand and arm starts the swinging movement and the body *responds* by turning to *assist* (not cause) the swing. Understanding of this is vital.

I warn you again. If the takeaway is started by a turn and dip of the shoulders you will not achieve the correct takeaway line . . . and consequently the alignment of your swing plane will be wrong.

ESSENCE OF THE TAKEAWAY

To understand the nature of the takeaway think of the simple chip shot. In it the backswing is performed entirely with THE HANDS AND ARMS. No body or shoulder action is involved. If the shoulders turned at all the club would be taken off the line. It is the same with other shots, and this is the KEY TO THE START OF FULL SHOT. Start the drive as you would start the chip . . . with the left hand and arm alone. Then add the body movement (the shoulder turn) at the proper time simply to allow the swing to progress further, clear to the top.

THE FULL SHOT IS MERELY AN EXTENSION OF THE CHIP, WITH THE SHOULDER AND BODY TURN ADDED SIMPLY TO PERMIT THE SWING TO PROGRESS FULLY.

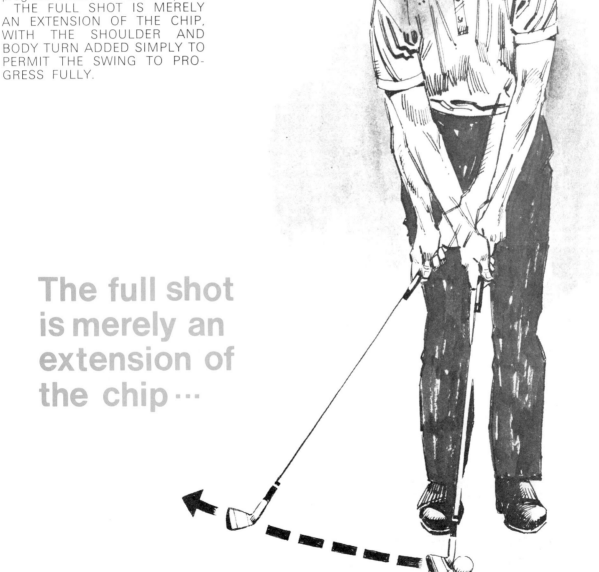

The full shot is merely an extension of the chip···

A correct takeaway line creates a correct swing plane···

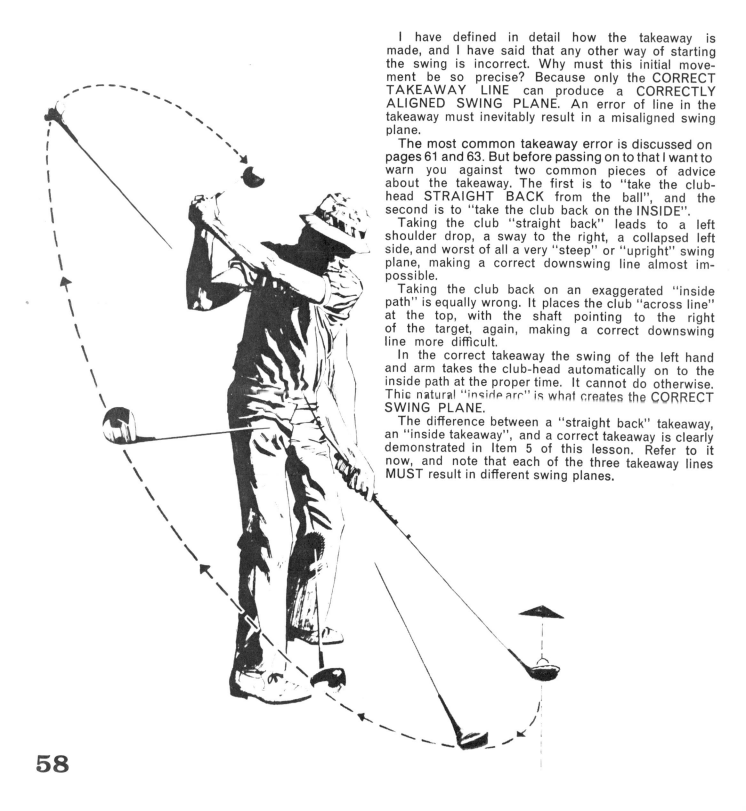

I have defined in detail how the takeaway is made, and I have said that any other way of starting the swing is incorrect. Why must this initial movement be so precise? Because only the CORRECT TAKEAWAY LINE can produce a CORRECTLY ALIGNED SWING PLANE. An error of line in the takeaway must inevitably result in a misaligned swing plane.

The most common takeaway error is discussed on pages 61 and 63. But before passing on to that I want to warn you against two common pieces of advice about the takeaway. The first is to "take the club-head STRAIGHT BACK from the ball", and the second is to "take the club back on the INSIDE".

Taking the club "straight back" leads to a left shoulder drop, a sway to the right, a collapsed left side, and worst of all a very "steep" or "upright" swing plane, making a correct downswing line almost impossible.

Taking the club back on an exaggerated "inside path" is equally wrong. It places the club "across line" at the top, with the shaft pointing to the right of the target, again, making a correct downswing line more difficult.

In the correct takeaway the swing of the left hand and arm takes the club-head automatically on to the inside path at the proper time. It cannot do otherwise. This natural "inside arc" is what creates the CORRECT SWING PLANE.

The difference between a "straight back" takeaway, an "inside takeaway", and a correct takeaway is clearly demonstrated in Item 5 of this lesson. Refer to it now, and note that each of the three takeaway lines MUST result in different swing planes.

The wrists must not roll during the takeaway

We have now got the club moving back from the ball on a correct line. This will automatically place us on the swing plane that we desire.

Now we must look at another takeaway error which seriously affects accuracy. It is the matter of wrist rolling.

The vast majority of players roll their wrists "open' or' "closed" during the takeaway, thus altering the alignment of the face of the club to the ball. The club face was square at address, and it must REMAIN SQUARE THROUGHOUT THE SWING. Then, when it is returned to the ball at impact it will STILL BE SQUARE, or at right angles to the intended line of flight.

So let's start with a guiding principle. It is this.
DURING THE TAKEAWAY, THE CLUB-FACE MUST BE AT RIGHT ANGLES TO THE SWING PATH AT ALL TIMES.

By "club-face" I mean the leading edge of the club.

By observing this simple rule, wrist rolling can be avoided.

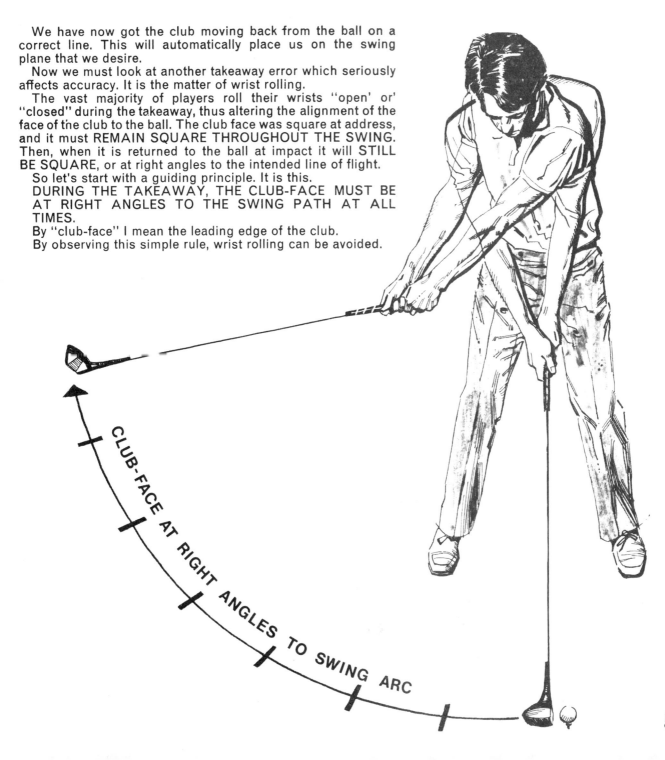

CLUB-FACE AT RIGHT ANGLES TO SWING ARC

Halfway back, club-face check

CLOCKWISE
WRIST-ROLL

open

shut
ANTI-CLOCKWISE
WRIST-ROLL

At the halfway stage of the backswing the club face will be vertical (as illustrated) if no wrist rolling has taken place.

Clockwise roll will place the club-face "open" at this stage.

Anti-clockwise roll will place the club in the "shut" position, that is "looking at the ground".

From the correct, "square", position at the halfway stage, the left hand and arm will swing to the top, placing the face at the correct angle at the top of the swing (see page 35).

The other two positions (open and closed) will result in an incorrect club-face angle at the top, and unless some correction is made in the downswing the blade will also be mis-aligned at impact . . . and inaccuracy is bound to result.

60

An incorrect takeaway. Causes and effects···

There are two pieces of golfing advice which, in my experience, are guaranteed to ruin the takeaway. They are "hold the club-head low to the ground in the takeaway" and "take the club-head, hands, arms and shoulders back in ONE PIECE".

We have seen that the takeaway is NOT "one piece". The hands and arms start the movement. Then the shoulders begin to turn to allow this swing to continue to the top. This implies a genuine SWING of the left hand and arm.

In the "one piece takeaway" the club, hands and arms are being set in motion by the turning of the shoulders. This is what I call the "body propelling the hands and arms". This is not a swing at all. It is a stiff, locked movement which actually destroys totally the swing of the left hand and arm. It leads to a lot of errors, as we shall see.

Attempting to "hold the club low to the ground" in the takeaway is supposed to give a player a "wide arc". In fact, it does the reverse. In trying to hold the club "low to the ground" the left arm reaches back, and down . . . and the left shoulder dips down with it. This brings about the collapse of the left side and a downward drop of the head (see illustration). Again, any possibility of a left hand and arm swing is destroyed. Now, with the arm swing blocked by the body, a player must look to his wrists to keep the club-head moving. This early wrist break completely destroys any chance of a "wide arc".

This type of bad takeaway is extremely common. Try to understand it, and compare it with the correct takeaway described on pages 56, 57 and 58.

The hands and club are being moved by body action

61

right

The left shoulder does NOT drop···

In a correct takeaway, the left hand and arm SWINGS THE CLUB back from the ball. The shoulders then begin to turn so that the swing can continue FREELY TO THE TOP. In this type of movement, the LEFT SHOULDER DOES NOT DIP DOWN toward the ground. Why should it? The left hand and arm is SWINGING FREELY FROM THE SHOULDER, and therefore the left shoulder MAINTAINS ITS HEIGHT FROM THE GROUND more or less constant.

This type of takeaway swings the club smoothly into the correct swing plane that we desire. Note again that there has been no CONSCIOUS attempt to "steer the club-head inside". It has moved "inside" quite automatically, and at the proper time. Indeed, where else could it go?

A typical
bad takeaway

Here again, we see the incorrect takeaway described earlier, but from a different angle. THE TURN OF THE SHOULDERS IS CAUSING THE MOVEMENT OF THE CLUB. This is obvious. Notice how the left shoulder is dropping down! Again I say, this is not a SWING . . . it is a "body heave" to set the club in motion. Above all, notice that this type of takeaway creates an ENTIRELY DIFFERENT TAKEAWAY LINE and leads to AN ENTIRELY DIFFERENT SWING PLANE. This is bound to lead to complications at the top of the swing.

This type of takeaway action causes two other faults. As the shoulder dips down the RIGHT LEG STRAIGHTENS. Remember, I said the right leg MUST maintain its FLEXED position if a full, correct turn is to be achieved.

Again, as the left shoulder dips down, the RIGHT HIP RISES UP as it goes back. This is proof that the body is being rocked sideways, rather than TURNING as it should.

In a correct turn, the RIGHT HIP MOVES BACK, BUT IT MUST NOT BE ALLOWED TO RISE UP. Like the left shoulder, it maintains a more or less constant height from the ground. The flexed right leg makes this possible.

A left shoulder drop
alters the swing plane

wrong

63

An incorrect takeaway leads to error at the top···

I want to warn you again about "taking the club straight back from the ball" and taking the club back "on the inside". As we have seen, in a correct takeaway the club swings quite automatically on to an "inside path". No special effort is required to place it there.

It is very important to appreciate that a correct takeaway, a deliberate "inside takeaway" and a "straight back" takeaway produce entirely different swing planes, and therefore different positions at the top.

These three drawings illustrate this point.

I say again, make no attempt to CONSCIOUSLY take the club back on the "inside", and disregard advice about taking the club "straight back" from the ball. Both are wrong!

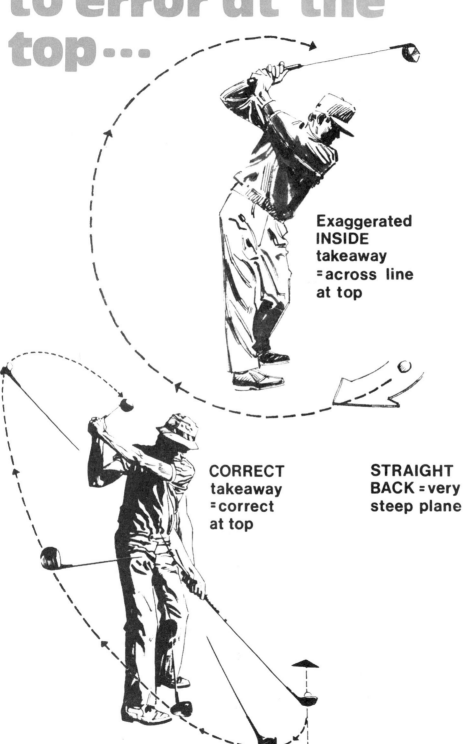

Exaggerated INSIDE takeaway = across line at top

CORRECT takeaway = correct at top

STRAIGHT BACK = very steep plane

The body turns simply to permit the left hand and arm swing to progress freely to the top

A full body turn in the backswing is a must for good golf. It is often stated that a full turn is necessary for "power" but we have already seen that this is a fallacy. Misleading advice about "coiled up power in the body" and "winding up the body muscles in the backswing" merely encourages heaving with the body during the entire swing.

A FULL TURN IS NECESSARY SO THAT THE CLUB CAN BE PLACED INTO A POSITION AT THE TOP FROM WHICH IT CAN MOVE DOWN INTO THE BALL, ALONG THE IN-TENDED LINE OF FLIGHT.

A FULL TURN is vital to correctly position the club at the top

But it is not enough merely to turn the shoulders. The RIGHT SIDE OF THE BODY, from hip to shoulder, must be fully cleared to the rear to achieve the full turn that we desire. And as the right hip goes back IT MUST NOT BE ALLOWED TO RISE UP. If it does, the right leg is straightening. Remember we said in Lesson 1 that the right leg remains *flexed* throughout the backswing.

And the left shoulder must not be allowed to DROP OR DIP. This is vital. Recall what we said about the first movement of the takeaway. It was made by the left hand and arm . . . then the shoulders began to turn. THIS MOVEMENT DOES NOT CALL FOR A DROP OF THE LEFT SHOULDER. Quite the reverse. The left shoulder must move across MAINTAINING A CONSTANT HEIGHT FROM THE GROUND if a full left hand and arm swing is to be achieved.

I mentioned the importance of fully clearing the right side. In order to do this most players will find it necessary to slightly raise the left heel. A left foot that is glued flat to the ground is certainly going to inhibit a full turn . . . the consequences of which you already know!

This is how a correct body turn progresses. After the initial movment by the left hand and. arm the shoulders begin to turn. Then the right side of the body begins to clear to the rear (over a flexed right leg) to assist the shoulder turn. Then the left heel rises so that the turning movement can be completed. In other words the body turn in the backswing OCCURS FROM THE TOP, DOWN, in the sequence 1, shoulders, 2. hips, 3. feet. Remember that, because the downswing occurs, logically, in the reverse order, namely, feet first, hip shift next and shoulders last.

Now that we understand the reason for the body turn and realise that it has NOTHING TO DO WITH GENERATING POWER, we can examine the mechanics of the turn in greater detail and really perfect the movement.

The role of the body

I hope you have already grasped the importance of the SWINGING OF THE LEFT HAND AND ARM in the golf swing. It is really astonishing that this simple truth has been overlooked in the long history of intensive golf instruction.

As you will know, teachers and players alike have assumed that "power in the golf swing originates in the body and is TRANSMITTED to the club via the hands". I consider this concept is profoundly incorrect and requires correction. I will explain later why so many great players have sincerely advanced this mistaken point of view. For the moment, I simply ask you to accept that it is an incorrect analysis.

I am quite sure, after almost forty-five years of teaching and study that this concept has ruined thousands upon thousands of golf swings . . . and continues to arrest the progress of pro's and amateurs alike.

So if power does not "originate in the body", what is the role of the body in the golf swing?

I have said that the SWING OF THE LEFT HAND AND ARM IS PARAMOUNT in the golf action. I stand by that. But this swing cannot occur if the body turn is incorrect! Therefore, the body must be trained to carry out the movements that make a FULL, FREE SWING OF THE LEFT HAND AND ARM possible.

Misuse of the body (an incorrect turn) destroys the capacity of the left hand and arm to swing. Conversely, a correct body movement CREATES THE CONDITIONS for a full swing of the left hand and arm TO MAXIMUM LEVERAGE. The correct body movement and the left hand and arm swing are COMPLIMENTARY. We cannot have one without the other.

Here is a point about which I am adamant. THE LEFT HAND AND ARM IS NOT PROPELLED BY THE BODY AT ANY TIME IN THE SWING. Or, putting it another way we don't turn the body IN ORDER TO MOVE the hand and arm.

THE LEFT HAND AND ARM SWINGS THE CLUB, and the body turns in order to ASSIST this swing and PROMOTE arm leverage. IT IS VITAL TO UNDER-STAND THIS POINT.

THE LEFT HAND AND ARM SWINGS THE CLUB IN THE GOLF ACTION. Body action must never hinder, or worse still, TAKE OVER, the role of the left hand and arm. The body turns in a controlled, "shaped" manner . . . not to move the left hand and arm . . . but to ALLOW IT TO SWING UNRESTRICTED in both backswing and downswing. This is what I mean when I talk of the body "responding".

I have made this point in some detail to answer critics who suggest that I advocate a swing of the left hand and arm ALONE, ignoring the contribution of the body to the swing.

If I have overstressed the role of the left hand and arm in the swing, it is because the accent in current golf teaching is very firmly on the body action . . . and particularly the assertion that "body movement CAUSES THE MOVEMENT OF THE HANDS AND CLUB" . . . it alone accounts for the vast number of poor golfers in the world today.

The left hand and arm is NOT propelled by the body at any time in the swing

As the left arm swings the club UP, the body stays DOWN

It is now time to refer to a matter of great importance in the golf swing. It is the phenomenon of "resistance" or "counter forces" in the golf action.

It is customary to talk of "the resistance of the hips to the turn of the shoulders in the backswing", etc. I have said there is NO RESISTANCE in the hips. Quite the contrary, the right hip and right side must be FULLY CLEARED TO THE REAR to assist a full shoulder turn. A full 45 degree turn of the hips must take place.

I am more concerned with a sensation that takes place in the "up" and "down" directions in a correct swing. It is this . . .

AS THE LEFT HAND AND ARM SWINGS THE CLUB BACK AND UP IN THE BACKSWING, THERE IS A DISTINCT FEELING (PARTICULARLY IN THE KNEES AND FEET) THAT THE BODY IS STAYING DOWN. THERE IS A DOWNWARD PRESSURE THROUGH THE FEET.

This pressing of the feet INTO THE GROUND INCREASES THE LEVERAGE DEVELOPED BY THE LEFT HAND AND ARM as it swings upward.

Once let the body RISE UP as the left hand and arm SWINGS UP, and the capacity of the left hand and arm to swing is immediately destroyed.

We will encounter this "resistance" again in the downswing, where it plays an equally important role.

Remember that any hint of "upward lift" or sway in the body during the backswing literally "takes the power" out of the left hand and arm swing. You can try this movement without a club in your hand. Swing the left hand and arm UP, at the same time sensing that the body remains DOWN. NEVER "GO WITH" THE SWING of the left hand and arm!

This is yet another example of the body acting to ASSIST the swing of the left hand and arm.

The role of the legs and feet in the backswing

The flexed right leg

I said in Lesson 1 that both legs are flexed at address, and the *right leg* must remain so flexed throughout the backswing movement. This is a *must* for a correct body turn. First, by maintaining a flexed right leg the head is held at a *constant height* from the ground during the backswing. It does not bob up and down.

Next, the flexed right leg promotes a full and correct body turn. By remaining flexed and active the right hip and side can be fully cleared to the rear in the way we have been describing. Remember, during the turn the right hip goes back, but it must not be allowed to *rise up*. If the right leg straightens during the backswing a full hip and shoulder turn will be virtually impossible. Further, the head will tip over in the direction of the target and the "shape" of the body turn is destroyed . . . as is the plane of the backswing. If this happens the club is *bound* to be out of position at the top.

Finally, the flexed right leg steadies the body and enables it to turn in the right way. By turning correctly the body *makes possible* a full, free swing of the left hand and arm. If the club is being moved by a body sway or a heave, the arm swing is destroyed. A correctly "shaped" body movement promotes a full and free left hand and arm swing. Club-head motion must *either* be supplied by the body *or* the left hand and arm. IT CANNOT BE BOTH!

The flexed right leg during the backswing promotes the type of turn that *assists* and promotes a full swing of the left hand and arm. The straight right leg destroys the turn . . . and with it the left hand and arm swing.

69

The position of the right leg remains unchanged throughout the backswing

Once the right leg has been correctly set at address its position remains virtually unchanged throughout the backswing. The body turn, in fact, takes place over the flexed right leg. By so "supporting" the swing, sway is prevented and a real TURN can take place.

Note that the right knee is "inside" the foot. It remains "inside" throughout the backswing. It must not be allowed to wander out to the right during the turn. This is a symptom of the sway we are trying to avoid.

Neither is there a marked "weight shift" from the left foot to the right foot during the backswing. At the completion of the backswing the weight is still more or less EVENLY DISTRIBUTED between the feet, just as it was at address. Remember what we said about raising the left heel? There, the weight was transferred to the big toe joint of the left foot.

It is the foot rolling movement which transfers most of the weight to the right leg during the backswing . . . and I have already warned you against foot rolling and swaying.

In the backswing the weight is concentrated on the INSIDES of the balls of the feet. There is a slight "knock kneed" feeling at all times, just as there was at address.

To develop and sense the "supporting" role of the flexed right leg in the backswing I often tell pupils to place a golf ball under the outside of the right foot. This transfers the weight to the inside . . . where it should be . . . and the vital stabilising task of the right leg in the backswing becomes clear. Try it, and note the "firming" effect it has on the backswing movement.

The right knee must NOT stray outward during the turn

The left heel must rise to permit a FULL body turn

We have seen that a really full body turn is necessary to permit the club to reach a correct position at the top of the swing. During the turn a player must make a special effort to CLEAR the right side of the body, from hip to shoulder, TO THE REAR. This permits a full 90 degree turn of the shoulders.

In clearing the right side as I have described most players will find it necessary to SLIGHTLY raise the left heel off the ground. This heel movement permits that little bit of EXTRA body turn which ensures that the club reaches a correct position at the top. Only the most supple players are able to execute a full body turn without raising the left heel. Consequently I build this movement into the swings of my pupils whether they feel the need for it or not.

Remember, in a full turn the hips move through 45 degrees and the shoulders through 90 degrees. Less than this is simply not acceptable! This left heel movement ensures that A FULL BODY TURN will be achieved.

INACTIVE FEET

Another reason why I encourage the left heel movement is because it keeps the feet live and active. THIS IS VITAL FOR A CORRECT BACKSWING AND DOWNSWING. If the feet are inactive, and the left heel is glued to the ground, the chances are that you will fail to make a full turn. A "resistance" will remain in the right side of the body which will inhibit a full shoulder turn. Inevitably, the club is then "off line" at the top and an out-to-in downswing path will result. THE FEET MUST REMAIN ACTIVE THROUGHOUT THE SWING.

A word of warning about OVERDOING this left heel movement! Some players raise the left heel far too much during the turn . . . tipping the foot up on the toe. This is both harmful and unnecessary. Players who do this ARE LIFTING THE BODY UP DURING THE BACKSWING. This is wrong. You do not lift the body to raise the left heel.

As the left heel rises the weight moves forward on to the big toe joint and a slight forward movement of the left knee occurs. That is all. The body must NOT BE ALLOWED TO RISE UP as the left hand and arm swings the club to the top. Rather, the body must stay "down" to permit maximum leverage of the hand and arm.

Thus, excessive movement of the left heel . . . and the lifting up of the body associated with it . . . destroys the left hand and arm swing and leads to misuse of the body. Superfluous movement in the backswing, sideways swaying, and heaving with the shoulders in the downswing also result. Unwanted movement in the backswing usually leads to unwanted movement in the downswing.

Study this illustration carefully, noting that the HEEL ALONE has risen slightly. The rest of the foot is firmly in contact with the ground. I am NOT advocating an inward roll of the left foot! As the left heel rises the weight moves FORWARD on to the big toe joint of the left foot, and is thus concentrated mainly on the inside of that foot. Thus, the left foot "breaks" at the toe joints. This is not the same as rolling the foot inwards! Again, study the drawing carefully and perfect this left foot movement. A correct foot movement promotes a correct "shape" in the body turn. A bad foot movement ruins the shape of the turn.

As the left heel rises, the foot does NOT roll inwards. It 'breaks' at the toe joints.

Inward rolling of the left foot in the backswing is in fact part and parcel of the "down and round" action that we are trying to avoid. The left shoulder drop causes a sway to the right, straightening the right leg . . . and the left foot responds to this sway by rolling inwards. This type of movement is a rocking motion of the body rather than a genuine turn.

If your turn is correct the left foot will "break" in the way I have described. If you are merely rocking the body sideways your left foot will roll inwards.

Check this left foot movement and understand it.

At the top

TOP OF THE SWING ANALYSIS

We have said that the backswing is performed solely to place the club in a correct position at the top. Now let us define what is "a correct position at the top", and why it is so important.

First, let's recall that the shoulders are FULLY TURNED through 90 degrees, the LEFT SHOULDER has not dropped as it came round to meet the chin, the RIGHT SIDE of the body from hip to shoulder has been fully cleared to the rear, the hips have turned through 45 degrees, the RIGHT LEG is still flexed, and the left heel has risen slightly.

ALL OF THESE FACTORS HAVE ENABLED US TO REACH THE DESIRED POSITION AT THE TOP.

The shaft of the driver should now be about HORIZONTAL to the ground, and PARALLEL with the intended line of flight.

I said "about horizontal". With the fairway woods and the irons the shaft will not have gone back quite this far. It will appear to be "laid off", as we say. This is simply due to reduced wrist action with these shorter clubs, which is perfectly natural.

The point I want to stress is that the shaft MUST be parallel with the intended line of flight OR "laid off" BEHIND THE HANDS as described above. The shaft (of any club) must ON NO ACCOUNT point ACROSS the intended line of flight . . . that is, to the RIGHT of the target. This "across line" position at the top leads to endless complications in the downswing as we shall see . . . and is in fact the result of an incorrect backswing.

It is also unnecessary for the shaft of the driver to dip below the horizontal. This is "overswinging", and leads to loss of control in the downswing. The horizontal position is quite enough. Indeed, many top players don't swing this far back, and are "laid off" at the top in the manner described.

The 'laid off' shaft

IRONS 'laid off'

WOODS swing completed

What is meant by the "laid off" shaft and is it good technique? Here is the completed backswing with a medium iron and a driver. Note that the shaft of the driver is horizontal to the ground and parallel with the intended line of flight. The shaft of the iron, however, has stopped well short of the horizontal . . . and therefore appears to be "laid off" as we say. This is entirely correct.

The shaft of the driver reaches a near horizontal position simply because of the ADDITIONAL WRIST ACTION that naturally occurs with the longer clubs. The shorter distance shots are naturally more "firm wristed". That ALONE accounts for the different positions of the shafts.

It is important to realise that if the medium iron swing were to be completed its shaft would reach EXACTLY THE SAME POSITION as the shaft of the driver and the blade angles of both clubs would be IDENTICAL.

In short, both clubs are "on-line" . . . but one has gone back further than the other. Hence the laid off shaft with the irons is entirely correct.

Same turn

One final point. Many golfers are under the impression that the swings with irons and woods are different . . . and that there is less body turn with the medium irons. Both ideas are incorrect.

THE BASIC SWING ACTION WITH ALL CLUBS IS THE SAME. THE AMOUNT OF BODY TURN WITH ALL FAIRWAY CLUBS IS ALSO THE SAME. The difference in the position of the shafts is accounted for SOLELY by the additional, natural wrist-action employed when using the driver and longer clubs.

Take care not to RESTRICT YOUR TURN with medium irons. If you do, YOU WILL NOT REACH A CORRECT POSITION AT THE TOP.

74

Sure test of a correct backswing

Below, left, is the same correct position from another viewpoint. I want you to notice the "shape" of the player's body. The line down his back to his hip forms a CONVEX CURVE. The body curves slightly AWAY from the target. This CONVEX body shape when the club is at the top of the backswing is common to all good golfers . . . and is in fact the RESULT of a correct series of movements in the backswing.

Contrast it with the "CONCAVE" body "shape", below (right). Here, the player's body curves TOWARDS the target. This posture is the result of the incorrect body movement in the backswing.   This CONCAVE body shape when the club is at the top is perhaps the most common sight in golf, and is a sure sign of an incorrect action.

Check your body shape in a mirror. If it is slightly CONVEX you can be sure your turn is substantially correct. If it is CONCAVE . . . well . . . you have not grasped what has gone before.

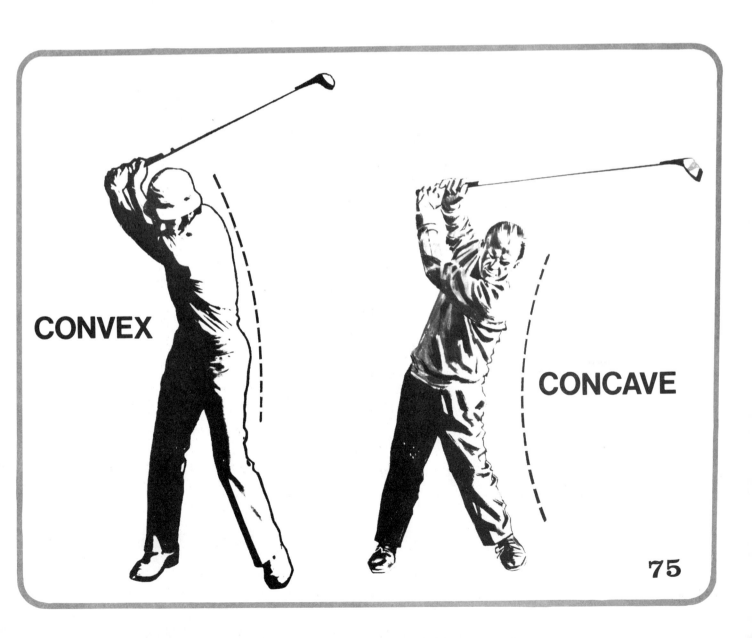

CONVEX

CONCAVE

75

'Across line' at the top... across line at impact

Here is the CONCAVE swing shape again, with the left shoulder drop, the straight right leg, and a right hip that has RISEN as it has gone back. This movement, as we have said, places the club shaft ACROSS LINE at the top.

The club-head, club shaft and hands are all OUT OF PLANE at the top. From here, only an "outside loop" (dotted line) down into the ball can result, leading to an impact ACROSS THE LINE OF FLIGHT. A swing down into the ball on the correct plane and line is virtually impossible without a major correction before the downswing begins.

It is an utterly hopeless position to be in at the top, and can be traced directly back to an incorrect takeaway, as we have seen.

Correct at the top ... 'on line' for the downswing

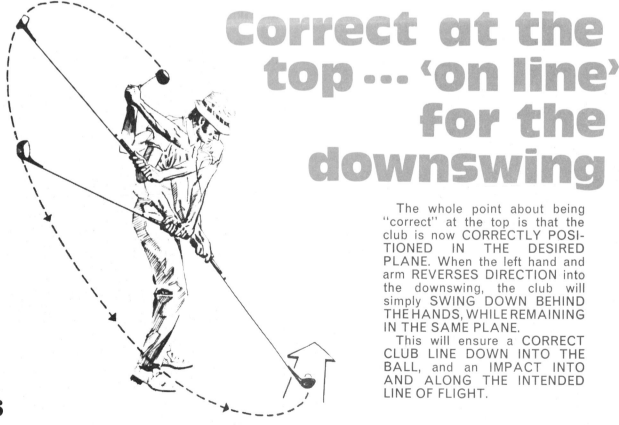

The whole point about being "correct" at the top is that the club is now CORRECTLY POSITIONED IN THE DESIRED PLANE. When the left hand and arm REVERSES DIRECTION into the downswing, the club will simply SWING DOWN BEHIND THE HANDS, WHILE REMAINING IN THE SAME PLANE.

This will ensure a CORRECT CLUB LINE DOWN INTO THE BALL, and an IMPACT INTO AND ALONG THE INTENDED LINE OF FLIGHT.

The angle of the club-face at the top is critical

If the grip is correct, and if there is no wrist-rolling (or other errors) in the takeaway and backswing, a correct club-face (or blade angle) at the top of the swing can be achieved. Then, when the club is returned to the ball in the downswing it will be SQUARE, just as it was at address.

However, if wrist-rolling does take place during the takeaway and backswing the blade angle at the top is bound to be incorrect. It will be either "open" or "shut". Then, a corresponding amount of wrist-roll will again be required in the downswing in order to "square' up' the blade at impact. This precision and delicate operation is obviously beyond the capacity of most players. Further, it is an unnecessary complication that can be avoided.

In a sound swing action the correct blade angle at the top is automatically achieved, ensuring a solid, SQUARE impact with the ball in the downswing. And this is what we want.

Below are the correct blade angles at the top with a driver and a short iron. Actually, the angles are IDENTICAL. If the swing with the short iron were to progress further, placing its shaft at the same angle as the driver, the leading edges of both clubs would be PERFECTLY ALIGNED.

Different shaft positions...SAME blade angle

77

The slightly 'cupped' left wrist···key to correct blade angle at the top

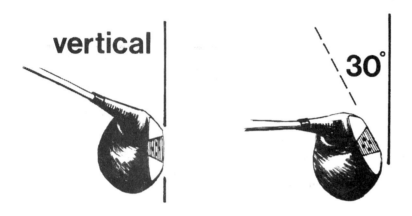

vertical

30°

The angle of the club face (or blade) at the top is governed by the angle that the back of the left hand makes with the left forearm. At the top of the swing the left wrist should be slightly "cupped". That is, the angle formed between the back of the left hand and the forearm should be about 30 degrees. This is ideal. This wrist position will place the club-face at a correct angle, namely (a) with the leading edge of the club VERTICAL or (b) inclined at an angle of about 30 degrees to the vertical . . . or somewhere between these two. All other angles at the top are incorrect and will lead to inaccuracy and loss of power.

open

Here, the angle between the back of the left hand and the forearm is MUCH TOO PRONOUNCED. The wrist is far too "cupped" and the club-face is consequently "open". I call this a "concave position" of the left wrist. It is extremely common among handicap golfers and tends to promote a slice.

shut

Here is the opposite extreme . . . a "convex" position of the left wrist. Note how the hand is dropped below the line of the forearm, "shutting" the blade. This hand position is comparatively rare among handicappers, and tends to promote a "smother" or a hook. A word of warning—you may see some top players employing this wrist position at the top. Don't be tempted to copy them! These "shut-faced" players combine this wrist position with a special type of body action in the downswing which enables them to return the club face to SQUARE AT IMPACT. Without this body action a monumental hook would result! Indeed, a hook is the constant enemy of all "shut faced" players. Don't flirt with this method!

correct

Here again is the correct left wrist position at the top . . . and the correct blade angle that goes with it. A slightly "cupped" wrist and a blade angle at about 30 degrees off the vertical. A correct grip, a square face at address, a free swing of the left hand and arm (without wrist roll) in the backswing, and a correct body turn COMBINE TO CREATE THIS POSITION.

A correct blade angle at the top coupled with a correct downswing movement (which we will examine in the next lesson) will automatically produce a DEAD SQUARE impact of club with ball, which is the secret of long, accurate shot-making.

Misuse of the right hand and arm

I am sometimes criticised for stressing the role of the left hand and arm AT THE EXPENSE OF THE RIGHT HAND. People have occasionally asked me if, in my view, the right hand has ANY role to play in the golf swing! My answer is this . . .

The vast majority of golfers grossly OVER USE THE RIGHT HAND in the swing. After all, most golfers are right handed and "right sided". They allow the strong right hand and side to DOMINATE THE SWING.

This, as we will see in Lesson 3, is FATAL!

It is the function of the LEFT HAND AND ARM that has been sadly neglected in golf teaching. I have merely tried to redress the balance.

I say again, A FREE SWING OF THE LEFT HAND AND ARM IS THE BASIS OF THE GOLF ACTION. The right hand and arm never acts independently in the swing. ITS PROPER ROLE IS ONE OF CO-ORDINATION WITH THE LEFT HAND AND ARM. The hands should WORK TOGETHER as a unit . . . WITH THE LEFT HAND IN CONTROL.

DURING THE BACKSWING THE RIGHT ARM AND ELBOW ARE VIRTUALLY PASSIVE, but the right HAND AND WRIST contribute toward control of the club-face at all times.

It is when the right hand and arm RESIST AND INTERFERE with the free swing of the left hand and arm that positional problems arise at the top . . . leading to complications in the downswing. The 'flying right elbow' (shown in this illustration) comes about precisely because the right hand is OVERPOWERING the left in the swing.

Lady golfers, in particular, tend to be VERY RIGHT HANDED. Their left arms are, not unnaturally, often extremely weak. Hence they actually SUPPORT the left hand and arm WITH THE RIGHT HAND at the top of the swing!

The solution to this problem is simple. THE LEFT HAND AND ARM MUST PLAY THE DOMINANT ROLE IN THE SWING AT ALL TIMES. If it does not, you have no alternative but to over employ the right hand.

THE RIGHT HAND CAN ONLY DOMINATE IF THE LEFT HAND AND ARM FAILS TO PLAY ITS CONTROLLING ROLE.

One final word of warning. Using clubs that are too heavy for you promotes misuse of the right hand.

'Overswing' is caused by overplayed wrist action in the takeaway

normal backswing

overswing

We have said that the shaft of the driver at the top of the swing should be horizontal or slightly short of horizontal. IT IS UNDESIRABLE FOR THE SHAFT TO DIP BELOW THE HORIZONTAL as this often leads to lack of control in the downswing. This unnecessarily "loose" swing is termed "overswing".

It is common for overswing to be attributed to "opening the hands at the top of the swing". I do not entirely agree with this. Admittedly the hands are opening . . . but why? All errors in the golf swing can be traced back to some cause. Nothing happens without good reason.

Overswing not only causes loss of control (and hence direction) in the downswing, but the excessive wrist action with it means that a consistent length of shot with the same club is impossible.

To be accurate, and score low, a player must hit a CONSISTENT LENGTH with each club . . . especially the irons. Overswing makes this virtually impossible.

cause, effect, cure.

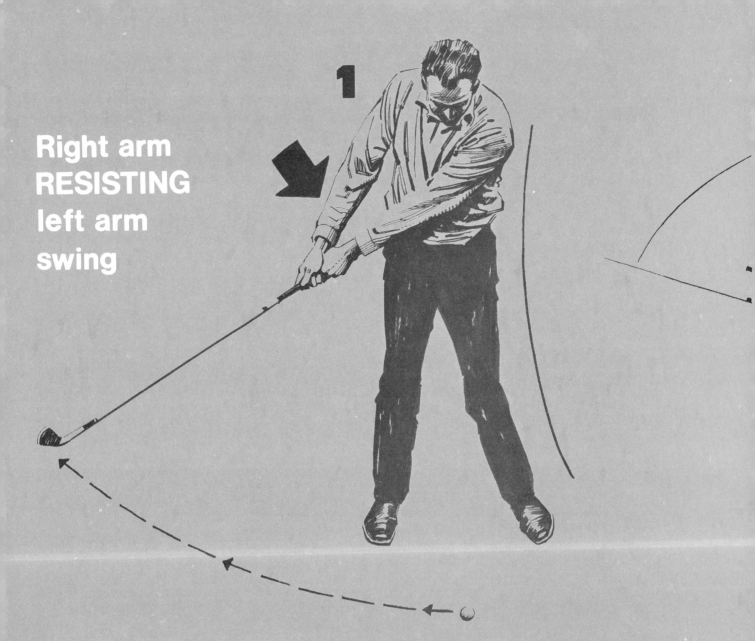

Right arm RESISTING left arm swing

1

The basic cause···a body action type takeaway

To understand the causes of overswing, let's consider an incorrect takeaway again. Here it is, with the left shoulder drop . . . and the CONCAVE body shape is appearing already. This is the result of "holding the club head low to the ground in the takeaway". There is absolutely no SWING OF THE LEFT HAND AND ARM AT ALL!

The left hand has gone back and DOWN . . . so the right forearm is DIRECTLY ABOVE THE LEFT . . . actually RESISTING any possibility of a left arm swing!

2

The left hand and arm swing is blocked, so the wrists MUST break early

Since the swing of the left hand and arm is now EFFECTIVELY BLOCKED both by the incorrect body movement and the resisting right arm, THE WRISTS MUST NOW BREAK IF THE CLUB-HEAD IS TO KEEP MOVING. This is precisely what happens. THE WRISTS BREAK TOO EARLY . . . AND TOO MUCH . . . actually destroying the "wide arc" that "low to the ground" is supposed to produce. This excessive wrist cocking accelerates the club-head to such an extent that the hands are literally FORCED OPEN as the club reaches the top. This opening of the hands is what causes overswing.

So we see that the hands DO NOT simply open at the top due to a loose grip as is so often stated. They are forced open by an incorrect swing action which leads to excessive wrist action. So to cure overswing we must first correct the swing action.

3

Cure. Really SWING the left hand and arm···

Overswing can be corrected simply by adopting the correct takeaway method outlined in page 58. If the left hand and arm STARTS the backswing movement . . . and if the shoulders turn IN ORDER TO PERMIT THE LEFT HAND AND ARM SWING TO CONTINUE UNRESTRICTED TO THE TOP there will be no REASON for premature or excessive wrist break to occur. It is as simple as that.

IF THE ARM DOESN'T SWING THE CLUB, THE WRISTS MUST. Remember that!

The wrists, incidentally, BREAK NATURALLY at the TOP OF THE SWING due to the momentum of the club-head. Hence, the shorter the shaft the less the club-head momentum . . . and the less the wrist break.

THE AMOUNT OF WRIST BREAK AT THE TOP WILL DEPEND UPON THE CLUB IN USE. Some wrist break occurs with the driver. Much less with the medium irons, and virtually NONE with the short irons.

I can recall at least one very good tournament professional who destroyed his future prospects by over-swinging. His excessive wrist break in the takeaway led to looseness at the top and inaccuracy at impact. He is now virtually unknown. Equally, I can recall only one top player with a very long backswing who remained an accurate striker of the ball.

FIRMNESS AND CONTROL AT THE TOP IS ESSENTIAL. It comes from getting to the top in the correct way.

If the arm doesn't swing the club, the wrists MUST take over !

We have already examined in detail the characteristics of a good backswing movement . . . and a bad one. Now, we see them side by side to make a direct comparison. Visual comparisons are a powerful aid to learning. Once the "picture" of a good backswing movement is established firmly in the mind correct execution of the movement becomes easier.

A full-length mirror is extremely useful for checking your body "shape".

Good and bad backswings. A comparison

1

The start of a bad backswing. The body is "propelling the hands and arms". Note that the player's head has already started to dip to the left. This is the first sure sign that the body is doing the work.

2

The effort being made by the body is now obvious. The upper body is "dipping down" to the left (bringing about the left shoulder drop) in order to move the hands and arms. The right leg is straight and the left foot is beginning to roll inwards.

3

At the top. The body "shape" is CONCAVE. The club shaft is "across line" at the top (pointing to the right of the target). The physical effort involved in this type of "body swing" is quite obvious. In fact, it can hardly be termed a swing at all.

1

The left hand and arm has clearly made the initial movement of the takeaway. The shoulders are now just starting to turn. This is the start of a GENUINE BODY TURN, and the left shoulder has MAINTAINED ITS HEIGHT FROM THE GROUND. The body is responding to the arm swing in a balanced, controlled manner.

2

The left hand and arm swing continues . . . the shoulders continue to turn in response. The head is STILL. The legs remain FLEXED. The right elbow is passive, and the arm is beginning to fold correctly BEHIND the left arm. The left heel is beginning to rise in response to the shoulder and hip turn. ABOVE ALL, THE HANDS ARE IN CONTROL OF THE MOVEMENT.

3

The POSITIONING movement is complete, and the club is "on line" for the downswing. The body has not "risen up" with the club . . . it has remained DOWN as the flexed knees indicate. Note the FULL SHOULDER TURN and 45 degree HIP TURN. No tension or effort involved here. Just a fluid, "shaped" body movement which has ENABLED the left hand and arm to SWING uninterrupted to the top.

Flat   or upright ?

UPRIGHT.
Club tends to
go forward,
OVER HANDS
from top

FLATTER.
Club stays
BEHIND HANDS
on the way down

There is a lot of discussion these days about whether the swing should be "upright" or "flat". My swing model results in a position at the top in which THE HANDS ARE NEARER THE RIGHT SHOULDER THAN THE BACK OF THE NECK. From this position, the hands can LEAD THE CLUB-HEAD AND SHAFT DOWN INTO THE BALL . . . which is a vital prelude to a correctly timed release of power...

as we shall see.

I do not favour the extremely upright position which is employed by many golfers at present. The upright swing and the "concave" body shape that we have condemned go together. It places the RIGHT HAND AND ARM IN A DOMINATING POSITION at the top of the swing. The right hand will thus TEND TO OVERPOWER the left in the downswing, leading to loss of club-line.

Further, from an upright position like this, maintaining the club square and "on line" through the ball, places great strain on the back.

In short, the "upright swing" tends to be destructive of club-line in the downswing, and leads to misuse of the body in the swing. Any movement that causes discomfort or strain should be avoided. It will lead to fatigue and inconsistency.

A bad swing analysed

Now that we have seen how a correct backswing takes place, let us examine the concepts and movements that sabotage a correct action. By understanding these errors we can avoid them.

First, as we already know, POWER DOES NOT ORIGINATE IN THE BODY. The body turn does not CAUSE the hands and arms, and the club-head to move. The body turn does not occur to "create power". The backswing itself IS NOT PERFORMED TO "GENERATE POWER". These concepts may be widely held and handed down from the "highest authority" . . . but that does not make them any more correct. We are going to see what happens to the swing when they are applied, and then test our own concepts against these old, false ideas.

Especially dangerous is the old cliché about "holding the club-head low to the ground in the takeaway". This is supposed to create a "wide backswing arc", but in fact it does the opposite!

Equally untrue is the concept of "the one piece takeaway". According to this theory the shoulders, arms and hands "start back together" . . . taking the club with them. Another way of saying that the body PROPELS THE HANDS AND ARMS!

This player thinks the backswing is for "generating power". He employs the "one piece takeaway" and he heeds the advice that "the club-head stays low to the ground in the takeaway". He also thinks that the shoulder turn STARTS THE SWING. Okay . . . let's see what happens.

Power is uppermost in his mind so he grips the club like an axe. Fully alerted for a massive effort his body lurches to one side to start the club-head moving. The club has only moved a foot but already HIS SWING IS RUINED. This is not going to be a swing at all . . . it is a body heave with wrist action added for additional force!

1

Holding the club-head low to the ground ··· a sure way to ruin a backswing

Now he thinks "low to the ground on the takeaway". The left arm extends backwards and downwards in obedience to the "law". The left shoulder dips down in response and the head drops with it. There is no sign of a turn yet, just a sideways rocking motion of the body! His "wide swing arc" theory has produced a king-sized sway. Note that the right leg is already straight and the left foot has begun to roll inwards. (See what I mean about the left foot roll and the sway being related?)

How about those arms and hands? Well, they're just hanging on to the club and going along for the ride while the body does all the work. Obviously this body dip can't go on forever or this chap will break in half. That's not a joke! Most "body action" players wind up with back trouble!

When the body dip does stop, how will the club-head keep moving? The wrists will take over . . . they will "break" prematurely in an effort to keep the whole show moving. Whatever happened to that "wide arc" that he was seeking? Now I ask you, did you ever see a top player make his takeaway like this? Yet millions of average golfers do, and they're the fellows who buy the instructional books!

See what I mean about good and bad concepts?

2

3

He's made it to the top . . . but what an effort! I call this a "coal-heaver's" action. It involves the use of terrific physical force to move a club that weighs but a few ounces! The "body swing" is clearly wasted power. How much easier and more productive to just swing the left hand and arm! The shoulders have turned at last . . . after a fashion . . . but just look at that body shape! I call this a "concave bow" . . . hallmark of the body heaver. Where can the club go from here . . . into and along the intended line of flight? I doubt it very much. Our "power man" has put the club up there with body action and he's sure to bring it down into the ball by the same method. We have here the classic conditions for a shoulder-roller's out-to-in smother, or slice, or hook, orbital shot, daisy cutter . . . you name it, it's possible! Any shot, except a STRAIGHT one. The odds against that are enormous. That's why this poor fellow suffers so. He is the victim of bad advice and I'm not really laughing at him. I feel sorry for him because he is keen, he wants to play good golf, and he's tying himself up in knots. Is this really the best that modern golf instruction can do for him?

By adopting correct concepts he could have a good action and be enjoying his golf, and employ a tenth of the physical effort in the process.

desired line & plane

Results of a bad backswing

This is the same fellow at the top seen from a different viewpoint. The circle represents the desired swing plane we were talking about. Our friend is nowhere near it! His body action has placed the club across line at the top. From there, he cannot possibly end up swinging along the intended line of flight through impact without a major correction before the downswing begins. He doesn't have the skill to make such corrections. Few of us do. The point is, he shouldn't be in this hopeless position in the first place.

This, I submit, is the result of well meaning but incorrect advice. This dreadful position can be seen any day, on any course or driving range. Why? Because the vast majority of players have read the SAME BOOKS and are consequently operating on the SAME FALSE PRINCIPLES.

You never saw a top player in any of the positions illustrated here, and yet the concepts which most of them advocate inevitably produce these results!

The only conclusion that one can draw from this analysis is that THE ACCEPTED CONCEPTS OF THE SWING DO NOT PRODUCE THE RESULTS they are INTENDED to produce. The swing MUST BE SEEN IN A DIFFERENT WAY. Not just for novelty, or to be controversial, but because golfers deserve better . . . and because golf is a great game.

After all, it was once thought that the sun moved round the earth. When that concept was reversed and corrected, we found we could devise a coherent model of the solar system, and then the universe.

Oddly enough, if you reverse many of the "accepted truths" of established golf instruction you come pretty close to the truth!

The golf instructional scene is as mixed up as that!

Poised for the downswing

We have now examined, step by step, how a correct backswing is made and what purpose it serves. The left hand and arm swings the club . . . the body turns in a "shaped", controlled manner to assist this swing . . . and the club arrives CORRECTLY POSITIONED AT THE TOP.

Again, I stress the word POSITION. So far, in both set-up and backswing we have merely been correctly POSTIONING THE CLUB AND BODY. The backswing movement has been controlled and unhurried. There is absolutely no need for force or speed.

Now that we are correctly positioned at the top, we can move into THE EXECUTIVE PHASE OF THE SWING . . . the downswing. From this correct position at the top the downswing is simplicity itself. If you are out of position at the top you are just storing up frustration for yourself!

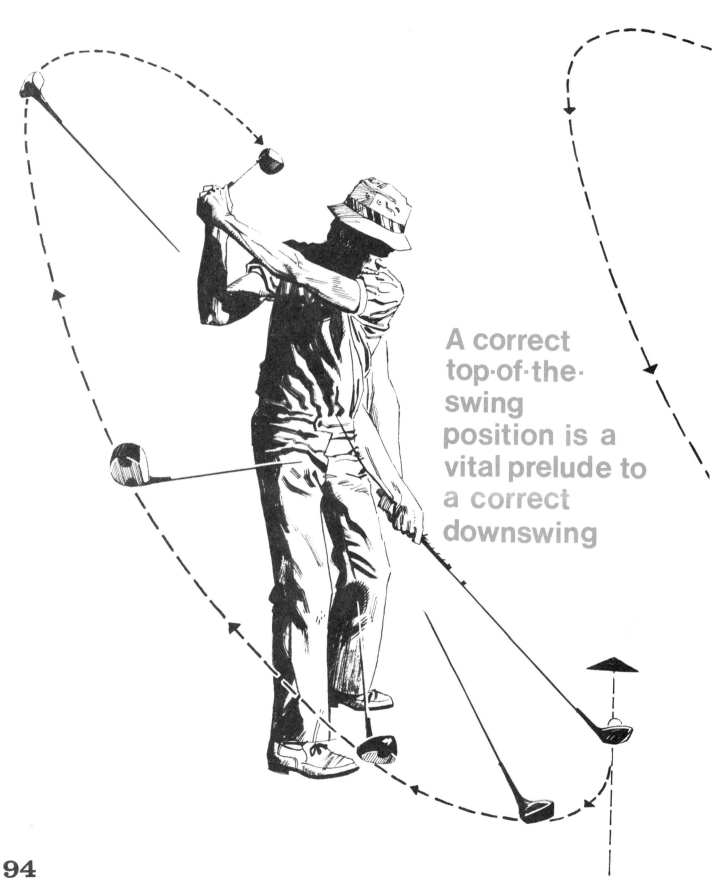

A correct
top-of-the-
swing
position is a
vital prelude to
a correct
downswing

The club has swung . . . on the plane . . . to the top. Now the left hand and arm SIMPLY REVERSES DIRECTION and swings the club down again . . . on the SAME PLANE, INTO AND ALONG THE INTENDED LINE OF FLIGHT. In the process of doing this the BALL IS STRUCK SQUARELY IN THE MIDDLE OF THE BLADE and is sent STRAIGHT on its way to the target. That, in the simplest terms, is what must happen next. We are about to see how it can be achieved.

It don't mean a thing if you ain't got THAT LEFT HAND AND ARM SWING! The accent is on SWING . . . and the SHAPE OF THE SWING. A good downswing consists of making a GOOD CLUB-LINE THROUGH THE BALL and RELEASING POWER WITH THE HANDS AT THE RIGHT TIME. A swing and a "release". Once think of "hitting" the ball and both the "swing shape" and a correctly timed "release" of power will evaporate.

POWER AND DIRECTION is what we want now . . . and that is what we're going to get!

An impact ALONG the intended line of flight ...the purpose of the golf swing

Downswing preview···

I have been saying throughout this course of instruction that MOST OF THE ACCEPTED AND WIDELY TAUGHT PRINCIPLES OF THE GOLF SWING ARE FALSE . . . and I have explained to you how this has come about.

There is more nonsense talked about the downswing, and how it is carried out, than any other phase of the swing movement. Almost every golf book ever written has described the downswing something like this . . .

"The downswing is started by a turn of the hips to the left. This sets the shoulders in motion, which sets the arms in motion, which sets the hands in motion. Then the hands deliver the clubhead into the ball with explosive force. It is a chain reaction started by the hip turn".

THIS ANALYSIS, OR ANYTHING LIKE IT, IS QUITE WRONG! It is an absolutely sure way to ruin an otherwise good swing.

I will give you an alternative to this misleading concept . . . . and many others . . . which will enable you to make a downswing which has both power and direction. I have seen my concept of the downswing transform long handicappers to single figure golfers in a year or two. Many of these have moved into the top ranks of amateur golf. A METHOD CAN ONLY BE JUDGED BY RESULTS, and I have seen my method transform players not once, but time and time again.

I will show you how to perform a downswing movement in which a swing into and along the intended line of flight IS ASSURED . . . time after time. This mechanical consistency is what golf is all about . . . and what leads to lower scores. Accuracy and power must be INHERENT in the swing action, and a player must be capable of repeating that sound action time after time.

We will see how this type of consistency is achieved.

My downswing concept (you will not be surprised to hear) is based upon a free swing of the left hand and arm down into the ball. A swing which occurs ENTIRELY INDEPENDENT OF THE SHOULDERS. We will see that the shoulders are kept out of the movement by FOOT AND LEG ACTION.

Once the shoulders are NEUTRALISED, the left hand and arm can MAKE A GOOD CLUB LINE down into the ball with mechanical precision, resulting in a square impact along the intended line of flight.

This club-line, combined with the "release" of the club-head by the hands at the PROPER TIME is what makes for long, accurate shot making.

So on to the downswing . . .

LESSON 3

LESLIE KING'S
famous
FREE ARM
SWING
method

REVIEW

The sole purpose of the backswing is to CORRECTLY POSITION THE CLUB AT THE TOP. The left hand and arm has swung the club up into position. In so doing it has created the swing plane. Now the left hand and arm must REVERSE ITS DIRECTION OF SWING . . . MOVING THE HANDS AND CLUB DOWN INTO THE BALL. As it does this, the HANDS, SHAFT AND CLUB-HEAD must REMAIN ON THE SAME PLANE THAT WAS CREATED IN THE BACKSWING . . . AND THE HANDS MUST LEAD THE CLUB-HEAD DOWN INTO THE BALL, CONSERVING POWER FOR A PROPERLY TIMED "RELEASE" AT THE BALL . . . AND NOT BEFORE! In short, we must maintain a good "club-line" down into and through the ball, and we must "release" the club-head at the right time.

A correct top-of-the-swing position is a vital prelude to a correct downswing

DIRECTION AND POWER   THE PURPOSE OF THE DOWNSWING

The backswing was performed to correctly position the club at the top of the swing. The purpose of the downswing is to achieve a POWERFUL, SQUARE IMPACT INTO AND ALONG THE INTENDED LINE OF FLIGHT. That is all.

Again, we have a concept of "club line", but to this we add a second factor . . . POWER. We want to hit the ball STRAIGHT . . . AND LONG.

THE CLUB MUST SWING DOWN FROM THE TOP ON AN ARC THAT WILL CAUSE IT TO AUTOMATICALLY SWING INTO AND ALONG THE INTENDED LINE OF FLIGHT THROUGH IMPACT AND BEYOND. This is the principle upon which a successful downswing is based.

In a correct downswing the hands, club-shaft and club-head MUST REMAIN ON THE PLANE AT ALL TIMES. Only then can the club-head end up SWINGING ALONG THE INTENDED LINE OF FLIGHT THROUGH IMPACT. If they stray from the plane, either above or below it, the club-head MUST ALSO STRAY FROM THE INTENDED LINE OF FLIGHT THROUGH IMPACT.

Thus, swinging down on the correct plane AUTOMATICALLY CREATES AN IMPACT INTO AND ALONG THE INTENDED LINE OF FLIGHT.

POWER

As to power, we are about to examine how it is achieved. As we do so it will rapidly become evident that developing power in the swing depends to a very large extent on SWINGING THE CLUB ON A CORRECT DOWNSWING LINE. We will see that POWER AND DIRECTION ARE CLOSELY RELATED. An incorrect downswing line tends to destroy power.

Further, there is no point in developing power if it is not combined with direction. We are simply knocking the ball FURTHER INTO TROUBLE! The idea of combining power with an accurately directed swing INTO AND ALONG THE INTENDED LINE OF FLIGHT is what we are now concerned with.

98

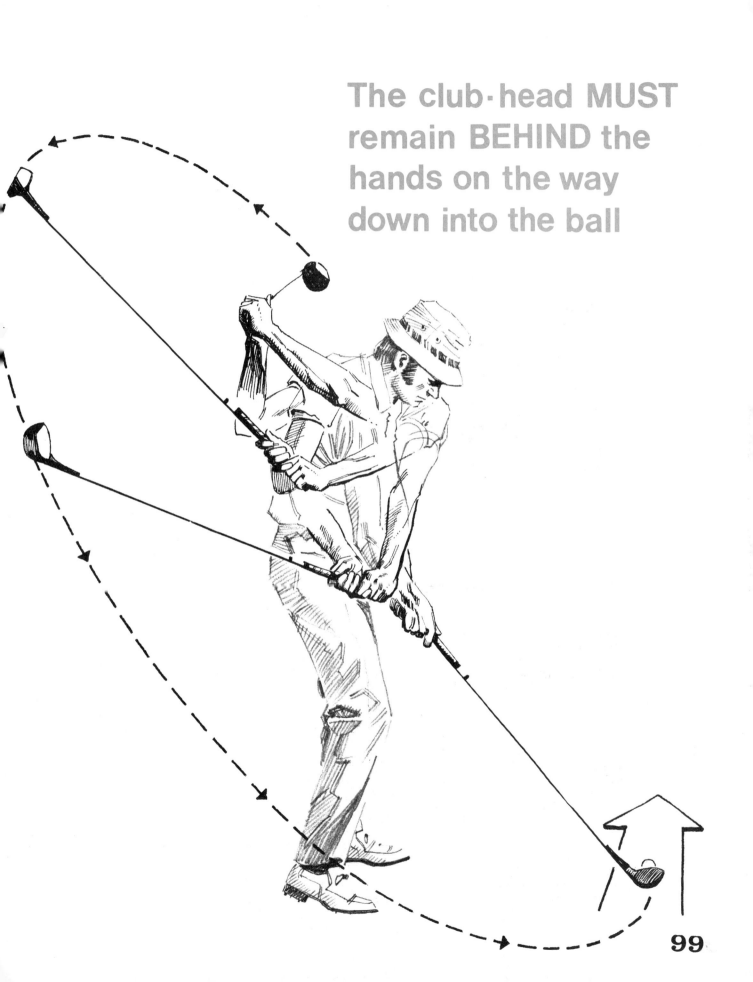

The club-head MUST
remain BEHIND the
hands on the way
down into the ball

The downswing problem

RIGHT
square

WRONG
open

The downswing is undoubtedly the most critical and misunderstood phase of the swing. It has been the subject of more misleading advice than any other phase of the swing movement. I intend to correct these errors, and replace them with concepts of the downswing that are both SIMPLE AND EFFECTIVE.

Essentially, the problem is this. MOST PLAYERS START THE DOWNSWING BY TURNING THE SHOULDERS. Consequently, they end up SWINGING ACROSS THE INTENDED LINE OF FLIGHT from "out-to-in", with the SHOULDERS OPEN AT IMPACT.

Why do they do this?. Because, I submit, the traditional analysis of how the downswing is performed TENDS TO PRODUCE THIS RESULT!

A correct downswing movement, as we have already said, MUST RESULT IN A POWERFUL SWING INTO AND ALONG THE INTENDED LINE OF FLIGHT. THROUGH IMPACT. For this to be achieved the SHOULDERS MUST BE SQUARE AT IMPACT, or better still, FRACTIONALLY "CLOSED". Keep this in mind!

Hence we see that PROPER CONTROL OF THE SHOULDERS

IS THE KEY TO A CORRECT DOWNSWING MOVEMENT. Indeed, we shall see that FOOT AND LEG ACTION in the downswing occurs largely to KEEP THE SHOULDERS PASSIVE AND UNDER CONTROL as the downward swing takes place. Hence my assertion that the DOWNSWING occurs from the feet . . . UP. I intend to explain this further.

For now, simply remember that without proper control of the shoulders both power and direction in the downswing will surely be destroyed!

100

Three downswing faults to be avoided···

Errors that ruin club·line

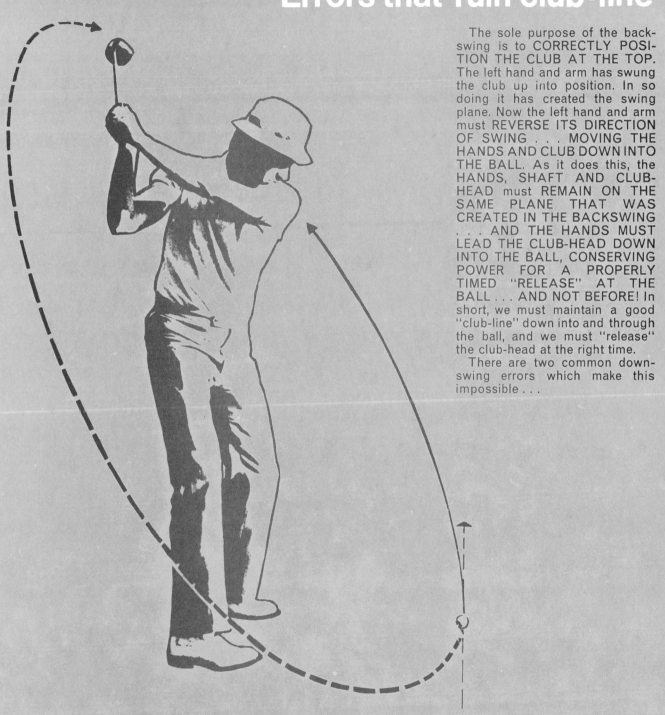

The sole purpose of the backswing is to CORRECTLY POSITION THE CLUB AT THE TOP. The left hand and arm has swung the club up into position. In so doing it has created the swing plane. Now the left hand and arm must REVERSE ITS DIRECTION OF SWING . . . MOVING THE HANDS AND CLUB DOWN INTO THE BALL. As it does this, the HANDS, SHAFT AND CLUB-HEAD must REMAIN ON THE SAME PLANE THAT WAS CREATED IN THE BACKSWING . . . AND THE HANDS MUST LEAD THE CLUB-HEAD DOWN INTO THE BALL, CONSERVING POWER FOR A PROPERLY TIMED "RELEASE" AT THE BALL . . . AND NOT BEFORE! In short, we must maintain a good "club-line" down into and through the ball, and we must "release" the club-head at the right time.

There are two common downswing errors which make this impossible . . .

1 Dominant right hand

Club thrown forward over hands···

Many pros and handicappers ALLOW THE RIGHT HAND TO DOMINATE THE LEFT AS THE DOWNSWING BEGINS. Control has been TRANSFERRED from the left hand and arm ENTIRELY TO THE RIGHT HAND.

Consequently the right hand throws the club-head FORWARD over the left hand and arm . . . COMPLETELY DESTROYING CLUB-LINE and RELEASING THE CLUB-HEAD FAR TOO EARLY.

The result. A weak, out-to-in impact!

FAULT CORRECTION

RETAIN CONTROL IN THE LEFT HAND AND ARM throughout backswing and downswing. The right hand will then assume its correct role.

OUTSIDE LINE

2 Turning the shoulders from the top

Club moves to an 'outside' line and an out·to·in impact ···

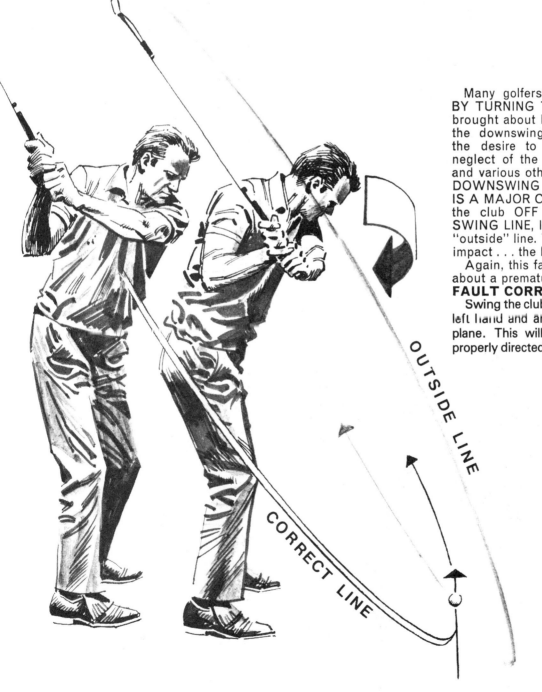

OUTSIDE LINE

CORRECT LINE

Many golfers start down from the top BY TURNING THE SHOULDERS. This is brought about by failure to use the feet in the downswing, an incorrect backswing, the desire to "hit" rather than swing, neglect of the left hand and arm swing, and various other errors. STARTING THE DOWNSWING BY TURNING THE HIPS IS A MAJOR CAUSE. The effect is to take the club OFF THE CORRECT DOWN-SWING LINE, looping it forward on to the "outside" line. The result is an across line impact . . . the hall mark of the "hacker".

Again, this faulty downswing line brings about a premature "release".

FAULT CORRECTION

Swing the club down into the ball with the left hand and arm, maintaining the correct plane. This will assist a correctly timed, properly directed release of power.

3 Throwing out from the top

The third common downswing fault is "throwing" the club-head out to the right as the downswing begins. THIS IS IN FACT A VERY EARLY RELEASE OF POWER. It is caused by over anxiety to "hit" the ball, and is often associated with a very fast swing.

A sure way to waste power!

POWER GONE BEFORE IMPACT

By releasing the power early, the club-head OVERTAKES THE HANDS BEFORE IMPACT making for a weak shot.

It is quite possible to "throw out" from the top and yet maintain a good line down into the ball. However, since power has been released early, it is almost certain that the point of release will VARY with each swing. Hence, shots WITH THE SAME CLUB will vary in length as the point of "release" varies. A caddie will find it very difficult to club you correctly. In short, throwing-out makes for weak shots of variable length. It also causes hitting the ground before the ball is struck.

FAULT CORRECTION

Maintain the club-head BEHIND THE HANDS on the way down. Allow the downward swing of the left hand and arm to make the initial movement in the downswing, then, when the hands have been lowered to about hip height, release the club-head. NOT BEFORE!

The role of the right hand and arm in the downswing

Hand and wrist always 'live'… arm and elbow PASSIVE until the'release'…

Misuse of the right hand and arm is extremely common in the downswing. It can cause both loss of line down into the ball and a premature release of power. Both errors are highly undesirable.

Some critics have suggested that I have stressed the role of the left hand and arm at the expense of the right hand. I disagree. IT IS THE COMMANDING ROLE OF THE LEFT HAND AND ARM THAT HAS BEEN NEGLECTED IN GOLF TEACHING, and most golfers over employ the right hand and arm anyway!

I have already said that the hands CONTROL THE CLUB AT ALL TIMES. The hands work together while the left hand ASSUMES THE COMMANDING ROLE. When we are talking about "hand control", we are speaking mainly about the interaction between the fingers and wrists of the hands. THESE ARE LIVE AND SENSITIVE AT ALL TIMES.

From a correct position at the top of the swing, the left hand and arm swings the club downwards into the ball. Meanwhile, both hands are contributing towards control of the club-head IN THE FINGERS AND WRISTS. However, the right arm and elbow are PASSIVE until the club descends to about hip height. Then . . . when good club-line through the ball is assured, the hands are in position to safely "release" the club-head powerfully into the ball.

105

What happens when the right arm and elbow is activated from the top

Again, the club is thrown forward, OVER the left arm to an 'outside' line ···

If, through misuse of the right arm or elbow, the right hand is allowed to OVERPOWER the left before the release, power and direction is prejudiced. It then comes into the shot TOO EARLY, interfering with the guiding role of the left hand and arm . . . throwing the club off line.

As long as the left hand and arm REMAINS IN CONTROL, the right hand will play its proper part . . . at the proper time.

IT IS ESSENTIAL TO REALISE THAT THE SHAFT AND CLUB-HEAD ARE MAINTAINED BEHIND THE HANDS DURING THE DOWNSWING. When so positioned, the hands are SENSING AND ANTICIPATING THE RELEASE THROUGHOUT THE MOVEMENT. When the downward swing of the left hand and arm has brought the hands down into position for a FINAL RELEASE OF POWER INTO AND ALONG THE INTENDED LINE OF FLIGHT, it is at THIS POINT that the hands release the club-head into the ball in a properly timed delivery.

Premature use of the right hand both destroys a timed delivery (which is the secret of power), and destroys club line down into the ball, resulting in inaccurate and mis-hit shots.

A correctly timed delivery is, in the final analysis, what the golf swing is all about. Once the left hand and arm has successfully made the line down into the ball, the HANDS TAKE OVER FOR THE FINAL APPLICATION OF POWER.

Downswing Master Plan

THE FEELING OF A CORRECT DOWNSWING

We are correctly positioned at the top of the backswing. How can we convey the feeling of a correctly executed downswing? The answer is so simple it may well astonish you. It is this.

THE LEFT HAND AND ARM SIMPLY REVERSES DIRECTION AND SWINGS DOWN INTO THE BALL.

As the left hand and arm swings down, the player must have the FEELING THAT HIS SHOULDERS ARE REMAINING IN THE FULLY TURNED POSITION. This is absolutely essential if the left hand and arm is to make A CORRECT DOWNSWING LINE DOWN INTO THE BALL. Once the shoulders turn, the left hand and arm is thrown FORWARD AND OUTWARD on the classic out-to-in loop of the slicer.

THIS STILLNESS OF THE SHOULDERS AS THE LEFT HAND AND ARM SWINGS DOWNWARD IS AN ABSOLUTELY VITAL CONCEPT IN MY DOWNSWING MODEL. Once it has been mastered, accurate, powerful striking of the ball in the middle of the blade becomes a reality. The vast majority of golfers grossly misuse the shoulders in the downswing, and consequently NEVER ACHIEVE A CLUB LINE THROUGH THE BALL. Once the shoulders have been NEUTRALISED at the beginning of the downswing, a good club line can occur and a golfer can be transformed very rapidly.

Players who have developed the habit of turning the shoulders in the downswing will have difficulty in maintaining them STILL as I have just described. ANY HINT OF THE "SHOULDER

Left hand and arm swing combined with

108

TURNING ACTION" MUST BE COMPLETELY ERASED FROM THE DOWNSWING MOVEMENT. Only then can the left hand and arm swing down into the ball on an arc that will result in a SWING INTO AND ALONG THE INTENDED LINE OF FLIGHT. And without a true left hand and arm swing down into the ball, a correct "release" is impossible.

By keeping the shoulders OUT of the downward swing into the ball we can arrive at the ball CORRECTLY ALIGNED for a solid, square impact. I said you should have the "feeling" that the shoulders remain in the fully turned position during the downswing. When swinging the left hand and arm alone (with the right hand off the club) it is indeed quite possible to do exactly this . . . and this is a very fine exercise . . . but when both hands are on the club the shoulders will of course "square up" to the ball as the club comes into the hitting area. It is impossible and undesirable to try to prevent this. BUT THE FEELING THAT THE SHOULDERS REMAIN FULLY

TURNED IS NEVERTHELESS RETAINED.

By retaining this feeling we arrive at impact with the SHOULDERS SQUARE TO THE INTENDED LINE OF FLIGHT, or better still, IN THE PRE-SQUARE POSITION with the right shoulder slightly BEHIND the left.

OPEN SHOULDERS AT IMPACT ARE SIMPLY NOT ACCEPTABLE, and indicate that shoulder rolling in the downswing has taken place. It is quite impossible to make a correct club line through the ball if the shoulders are open at impact. It is also impossible to RETAIN POWER IN THE HANDS if this happens.

shoulder control

This downward swing of the left hand and arm which I have just been describing is of such great importance to a SOUND SWING ACTION that I want to explain it even more clearly before passing on.

IF THE LEFT HAND AND ARM DOES NOT MAKE THE MOVEMENT DOWN INTO THE BALL, THE SHOULDERS MUST. It is absolutely vital to understand this point. Thus, the only way to KEEP THE SHOULDERS OUT OF THE SHOT IS TO SWING THE LEFT HAND AND ARM FREELY DOWN INTO THE BALL.

Remember, so much depends upon keeping the SHOULDERS PASSIVE at this stage of the swing. If they remain passive we can (1) swing the club down to the ball on the desired plane . . . and hence on the correct line for a truly square, straight impact. (2) We can maintain the shaft and club-head BEHIND the hands on the way down. Opening the shoulders throws the club-head forward, thus wrecking the con-

ditions for a correctly timed release. (3) We can arrive at the ball correctly ALIGNED with SQUARE SHOULDERS for a really POWERFUL RELEASE into and along the intended line of flight.

IN OTHER WORDS, IF YOU EMPLOY THE SHOULDERS AT ALL IN THE DOWNSWING . . . EVEN JUST A LITTLE . . . good club line, a properly timed release and an on-line impact are all RENDERED IMPOSSIBLE. In short, the entire swing is ruined.

WRONG. shoulders opening!

RIGHT. shoulders still fully turned at start

What you should feel at the top···

Upward pressure from the ball of the left foot 'powers' the hands at the top

I said in Lesson 2 that the left heel must rise to permit a full body turn in the backswing, and that I built this left heel movement into the swings of my pupils whether they felt the need for it or not. I also said that there was NO MARKED TRANSFER OF WEIGHT TO THE RIGHT LEG in the backswing.

THE VITAL PURPOSE OF THIS LEFT HEEL RAISING . . . AND THE CONSEQUENT TRANSFER OF WEIGHT FORWARD ON TO THE BIG TOE JOINT OF THE LEFT FOOT is clearly sensed once we are at the top of the backswing.

WE SENSE THAT THE BODY IS IN PERFECT BALANCE DUE TO A SYSTEM OF CONTROL THAT ORIGINATES IN THE BIG TOE JOINT OF THE LEFT FOOT, PASSING DIAGONALLY UP THE BODY, TO THE SHOULDERS . . . AND FINALLY TO THE HANDS.

The Pressure felt on the INSIDE OF THE LEFT FOOT (under the big toe joint) is providing a base (a "resistance") for the downward LEFT ARM LEVERAGE that is about to occur. Indeed, the free downward swing of the left hand and arm CANNOT OCCUR WITH-OUT IT.

Power, conservation, release. A vital concept !

POWER

This upward "resistance" is what CREATES POTENTIAL POWER IN THE HANDS AT THE TOP OF THE SWING . . . power that will be released at the correct instant of time in the downswing. Hence, we can say that . . .

Downward drive *plus* Upward resistance *equals* POWER. The raised left heel thus CREATES POWER IN THE HANDS at the top.

We not only SENSE THE POWER IN THE HANDS, we also (thanks to the control imparted by correct use of the left foot) SENSE THAT WE CAN CONSERVE AND "RELEASE" THAT POWER AT WILL.

FOR THE FIRST TIME IN THE SWING MOVEMENT WE ARE AWARE OF THE POTENTIAL POWER IN THE HANDS . . . AND WE ARE CONSCIOUS OF THE FACT THAT WE HAVE THE NECESSARY CONTROL TO "RELEASE" THAT POWER AT THE CORRECT TIME.

Thus, the "body poise" at the top which is IMPARTED BY THE CORRECT USE OF THE INSIDE OF THE LEFT FOOT MAKES US (1) CONSCIOUS OF THE POTENTIAL POWER IN THE HANDS, it also gives us (2) A SENSE OF THE NEED TO CONSERVE THIS POWER FOR THE RIGHT PLACE IN THE SWING, and finally (3) we have a feeling of COMPLETE CONFIDENCE THAT WE CAN "RELEASE" THIS POWER AT THE RIGHT TIME AND PLACE IN THE DOWNSWING . . . AND THUS WE SUBCONSCIOUSLY SENSE EXACTLY WHERE THAT "RELEASE" POINT IS!

TIMING

This innate knowledge is what we are describing when we talk about "timing". It is not a "gift", or some sixth sense . . . it is a feeling of CONTROL AND CERTAINTY that arises out of a correct, sensitive series of body movements in the backswing.

AS THESE BODY MOVEMENTS ARE LEARNED AND ACQUIRED, SO TOO, THIS AWARENESS OF THE POTENTIAL POWER IN THE HANDS, and the need to "RELEASE" THIS POWER AT THE CORRECT TIME is developed. Once sensed, the matter of timing the "release" of power in the downswing is merely arrived at by usage.

Thousands of players, pro and amateur, go through their golfing lives with absolutely no sense of the POTENTIAL POWER IN THEIR HANDS AT THE TOP OF THE SWING. Consequently, they have never anticipated the next stage which is the release of that power at the right time.

The progress of such players must inevitably be arrested at some stage, since they have no awareness OF THE VERY ESSENCE OF THE SWING . . . THE PHENOMENON OF A TIMED RELEASE OF POWER WITH THE HANDS.

I stress again, this AWARENESS, and the priceless technical bonuses that flow from it IS ACQUIRED BY A SHAPED, CONTROLLED BODY TURN IN THE BACKSWING, AND IN PARTICULAR THE CONTROL AND SENSITIVITY THAT ORIGINATES IN THE BIG TOE JOINT OF THE LEFT FOOT WHEN THE HANDS ARE AT THE TOP OF THE SWING.

Starting down

Now that we have analysed in some detail exactly what we should feel at the top of the swing, we can move on to consider exactly how the downswing is carried out.

We now understand the truth of what I have been stressing right from Lesson 1. The backswing has nothing to do with "generating power", hence it is SMOOTH, UNHURRIED and STRAIN FREE. We are merely POSITIONING the hands, club and body CORRECTLY prior to the downward swing. Once correctly positioned (as a result of a correct series of movements) THE HANDS AUTOMATICALLY ACQUIRE . . . OR BECOME "CHARGED" WITH . . . POTENTIAL POWER AT THE TOP.

As we sense this power at the top the SWING SLOWS DOWN. Indeed, the transition from backswing to downswing IS THE SLOWEST PART OF THE SWING. This "slow down" at the top ACCENTUATES AND AMPLIFIES the feeling of CONSERVED POWER that we talked about earlier. We begin to ANTICIPATE the "release" . . . but at the same time WE STRONGLY SENSE THE NEED TO CONSERVE THAT POWER FOR THE FINAL STAGES OF THE DOWNSWING.

Now we realise that this feeling of power at the top DEPENDS UPON A PASSIVE, CONTROLLED BACKSWING. If, by applying force, we had sensed this power in the hands during the backswing itself we would have "jumped the gun" and "charged" the hands too soon. Hence, we would likewise "release" power too soon in the downswing, and nothing on earth could prevent it. In short, we would "lose our timing", hit from the top, throw the shoulders into the shot and DESTROY THE WHOLE MOVEMENT.

This impatience to "hit" is extremely common. It is a direct result of thinking about the backswing in terms of "generating power". The backswing is then performed by BODY ACTION rather than with a free swing of the left hand and arm.

Transition from backswing to downswing, SLOWEST PHASE OF THE SWING !

At the top we should have a clear sensation of the POTENTIAL POWER IN THE HANDS AND WRISTS . . . and an equally clear AWARENESS that the hands and wrists are IN CONTROL OF THE CLUB.

Now, MAINTAINING THE SHOULDERS IN THE FULLY TURNED POSITION, we simply commence the downward swing of the left hand and arm. That is how the downswing starts, and nothing could be simpler!

I stress again, THE SHOULDERS MUST REMAIN IN THE FULLY TURNED POSITION AT THE BEGINNING OF THE DOWNSWING! The same left foot action that has "charged" the hands with power is ENABLING US TO CONTROL THE SHOULDERS.

By keeping the shoulders fully turned the left hand and arm can SWING FREELY FROM THE LEFT SHOULDER, taking the club-head down into the ball ON A CLUB LINE that will result in a swing INTO AND ALONG THE LINE OF FLIGHT THROUGH IMPACT.

THE SHOULDERS ARE HELD IN THE FULLY TURNED POSITION AS THE LEFT HAND AND ARM BEGINS TO SWING DOWN.

The control imparted by the raised LEFT HEEL is the key to SHOULDER CONTROL and correct BODY POSITION at the start down ...

THIS ENSURES GOOD
CLUB·LINE THROUGH THE BALL···

Once let those shoulders turn . . . even just a little . . . at the beginning of the downswing and two errors are bound to result. You will . . .

1) Destroy club-line down into the ball by looping the club on to an "outside" path, and
2) You will destroy the ability to swing of the left hand and arm!

Here is an exercise that you can do to prove these two statements for yourself.

EXERCISE 1 CLUB-LINE

Take a club in your hands and assume the correct top of the swing position. Now, MAINTAINING THE SHOULDERS IN THE FULLY TURNED POSITION swing the left hand and arm slowly down NOTING THAT A CORRECT DOWNSWING LINE IS AUTOMATICALLY ACHIEVED. Repeat this several times.

RIGHT. Shoulders under control = good club·line

WRONG. Shoulders open = loss of club·line

Now, go back to the top, and this time ALLOW YOUR SHOULDERS TO TURN slightly as the left hand and arm swings down. NOTE THAT THE LEFT HAND AND ARM IMMEDIATELY MOVES TO THE "OUTSIDE" DOWNSWING PATH which must result in an out-to-in impact!

Thus, good club-line through the ball DEPENDS UPON THE STILLNESS OF THE SHOULDERS at the beginning of the downswing.

EXERCISE 11 "SEPARATION"

But there is a second result, which you may have sensed, which is very subtle and equally important. By allowing the shoulders to turn as the left hand and arm started down you ACTUALLY DESTROYED THE CAPACITY OF THE LEFT HAND AND ARM TO SWING! Did you feel that? You took the "power" out of the arm.

Remember how, in the takeaway, the freedom of the left hand and arm to SWING DEPENDED UPON A STILLNESS OF THE SHOULDERS AND AN ABSCENCE OF SWAY? If you had swayed to the right as your left hand and arm started back YOU WOULD HAVE DIMINISHED ITS SWING CAPACITY. We have

exactly the same situation here.

THE SHOULDERS MUST REMAIN STILL (in the fully turned position) TO ALLOW THE SWING OF THE LEFT HAND AND ARM TO TAKE PLACE. Move those shoulders, even fractionally, and you DIMINISH the capacity of the left hand and arm to swing.

`Separation´

The two vital points at which it occurs ···

take-away

start down

This ability of the left hand and arm to swing INDEPENDENT OF THE SHOULDERS I call "SEPARATION". Here is an exercise to develop "separation".

Take a club and assume the correct top of the swing position. Now, keeping the SHOULDERS FULLY TURNED, start the left hand and arm SLOWLY DOWNWARD into the ball. When the left hand and arm has moved downward for a distance of about a foot to eighteen inches . . . STOP . . . and return it to the top again. REPEAT THIS DOWN/UP MOVEMENT SEVERAL TIMES, keeping the shoulders IN THE FULLY TURNED POSITION.

What do you feel? You sense, perhaps for the first time, THAT THE LEFT HAND AND ARM CAN SWING ENTIRELY INDE-PENDENT OF THE SHOULDERS AND BODY. You realise that the arm is NOT PROPELLED downward by shoulder and body action. It SWINGS FREELY DOWN QUITE INDEPENDENTLY OF THE SHOULDERS.

THIS IS WHAT MUST HAPPEN IN A CORRECT DOWNSWING. Once the downward swing of the left hand and arm is under way, the body REACTS to this swing (we are about to describe this reaction) in what I describe as the "lateral shift". However, it is vital to realise that the body REACTS to the downward swing of the left hand and arm. THE BODY DOES NOT CAUSE THE DOWNWARD MOVEMENT OF THE LEFT HAND AND ARM.

Repeat this "separation" exer-cise often. It is the vital foundation of a correct downswing movement. Once perfected, the basis for a sound and powerful downswing is laid.

Again, we must guard against starting the downswing with "body action" . . . and that is what is happening if the shoulders are allowed to turn. Body propulsion and a free left hand and arm swing CANNOT CO-EXIST TOGETHER. It must be either one or the other. Hence, IF THE SHOULDERS TURN AT THE COMMENCEMENT OF THE DOWNSWING, THE FREE LEFT HAND AND ARM SWING IS DESTROYED. And if the left hand and arm is NOT making the downward swing into the ball A CORRECTLY TIMED RELEASE OF POWER WITH THE HANDS IS IMPOSSIBLE!

Correct left foot action maintains the shoulder turn to ENABLE separation to occur···

'SEPARATION'··· or how to make a genuine, free, left arm swing INDEPENDENT of the shoulders···

NOTE·The hands and wrists are in active **CONTROL** of the club!

SUMMARY

Hence, a correct start to the downswing depends absolutely upon MAINTAINING THE SHOULDERS IN THE FULLY TURNED POSITION while the LEFT HAND AND ARM STARTS THE DOWNWARD SWING. Three vital factors result from this . . . (1) The left hand and arm retains the CAPABILITY TO SWING. (2) Good club-line down into the ball is assured, and (3) a correctly timed "release" with the hands can be made.

I am sure I do not need to add that a downswing that begins with a conscious TURN OF THE HIPS TO THE LEFT cannot possibly achieve these three conditions! On the contrary, as the hips open the SHOULDERS ARE THROWN OPEN TOO . . . and a correct downswing is doomed from that moment on!

All that follows in the downswing depends TOTALLY upon real 'SEPARATION' being achieved at the START

The left hand and arm has started the downward swing while the SHOULDERS REMAIN IN THE FULLY TURNED POSITION. We sense the POTENTIAL POWER IN THE HANDS and we are conscious that the HANDS AND WRISTS ARE MAINTAINING CONTROL OF THE CLUB.

In Lesson 2, you will recall, we noted that there was more "wrist action" with the driver and longer clubs than with the mid and short irons. This was a matter of VARYING HANDS AND WRIST CONTROL according to the type of shot being played. The "wrist action" with iron shots was more restricted than with the drive and fairway wood shots.

Thus, the amount of "wrist break" required for any given shot is ESTABLISHED AT THE TOP OF THE SWING. Now, as the downswing begins, THAT SAME AMOUNT OF WRIST BREAK IS MAINTAINED BY THE HANDS UNTIL THE POINT OF "RELEASE". Thus, the club-shaft and the club-head are maintained BEHIND THE HANDS in the downswing for about HALF OF THE WAY DOWN INTO THE BALL. Or putting it another way, the ANGLE formed by the shaft and the left arm at the top of the swing is MAINTAINED until the point of "release". This I call "preserving the angle".

If that angle is INCREASED TOO SOON power is being released too early . . . AND IS WASTED. I discuss elsewhere the consequences of an "early release of power by the hands". I will simply say here that it results in weak shots of variable length with the same club. Your shots with, say a 5 iron will vary from 140 to 160 yards in length instead of being neatly grouped in a small area. Obviously this sort of distance variation will make it impossible for you to rifle shots close to the pin. IF THE POINT OF "RELEASE" VARIES, DISTANCE TOO MUST VARY.

I have already said that, given a correct backswing movement, a player will sense the power in his hands at the top of the swing. He will also sense the need to CONSERVE THAT POWER and "RELEASE" IT AT THE RIGHT INSTANT OF TIME. Thus, the matter of TIMING THE RELEASE, or IDENTIFYING THE PRECISE POINT OF RELEASE in the downswing is arrived at by repeating the action and, at first, perhaps consciously "feeling" for the correct release point. Later, as the precise point of release is identified, the action will become AUTOMATIC.

A controlled delivery of power…

The `release´

"PRESERVING THE ANGLE"

I want to stress here that when I am talking about "preserving the angle" I am NOT ASKING YOU TO CONSCIOUSLY "HOLD BACK" THE CLUB HEAD in the downswing. Thinking of a "late hit" is not the way to understand this movement. It will simply wreck it. Let me explain.

THE HANDS AND WRISTS ARE IN CONTROL OF THE CLUB AT ALL TIMES, and the INTENTION TO "RELEASE" POWER INTO THE BALL WITH THE HANDS is a fundamental thought of the downswing. Thus, thinking in terms of "holding back" is contrary to the CENTRAL PURPOSE OF THE DOWNSWING. We want to develop power, not hinder that development.

It is the intention to DELIVER POWER INTO THE BALL WITH THE HANDS that sets THE LEFT HAND AND ARM IN MOTION at the beginning of the downswing. But, as I have already said, we must "release" that power at the correct instant of time in order to achieve MAXIMUM ACCELERATION OF THE CLUB-HEAD AT THE MOMENT OF IMPACT. Not before . . . or after.

It is this "timing" of the release that causes the "angle" to be preserved. THE ANGLE HAS REMAINED CONSTANT BECAUSE THE MOMENT OF RELEASE HAS NOT YET OCCURRED.

You employ this instinctive skill every time you use a hammer. You do it SUBCONSCIOUSLY. Try to do it consciously and you will wreck the action. When chopping wood with an axe you do not CONSCIOUSLY RELEASE THE AXE HEAD in order to strike the log. Again, you do it INSTINCTIVELY.

IT IS THE SAME IN THE GOLF SWING.

The HANDS AND WRISTS RETAIN CONTROL OF THE CLUB, sensing and ANTICIPATING the "release". Thus, "preservation of the angle" is automatically achieved in a correct downswing. The angle increases when the hands and wrists perform the "release". Thus, a very early increase of that angle INDICATES A PREMATURE RELEASE WITH THE HANDS . . . AND LOSS OF POWER.

"Preserving the angle" is a RESULT of a properly timed "release". It is not a cause, as it is not an action that we can attempt to CONSCIOUSLY control.

A bad swing action may have dulled your sense of timing, and consequently your ability to make a correct "release". A correct swing action will soon restore your natural, instinctive sense of a correctly timed release. For a while, you will CONSCIOUSLY be "feeling" for the correct release point in your swing. But you will soon discover it, and then it will become a SUBCONSCIOUS action again.

It is when the left hand and arm FAILS TO INITIATE the downward swing that the hands and wrists are ACTIVATED TOO EARLY, throwing the club-head out in an "early release". That is why I said earlier that a properly timed release DEPENDS UPON a free downward swing of the left hand and arm.

Thus, we are not CONSCIOUSLY DELAYING anything, or trying to "hit late". We are correctly TIMING THE INSTANT OF RELEASE so that maximum power is developed at the MOMENT OF IMPACT. Not after . . . and certainly not before!

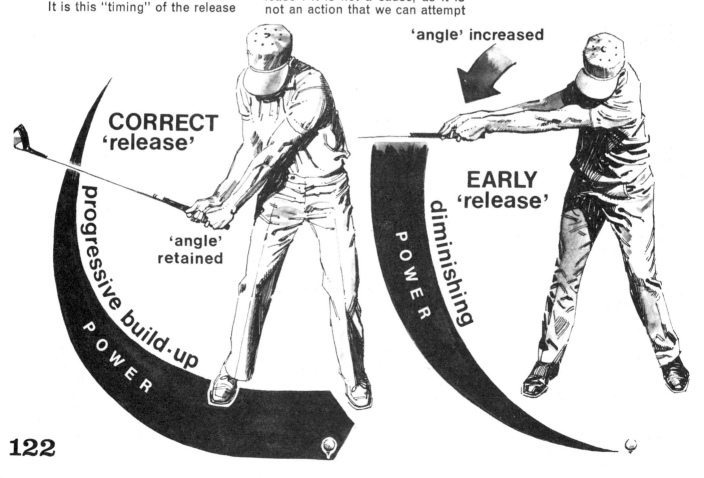

CORRECT 'release'
progressive build-up POWER
'angle' retained

'angle' increased
EARLY 'release'
diminishing POWER

A correct release requires TIME, not SPEED of swing !

Then the HANDS can retain control

SPEED OF THE DOWNSWING

The speed at which the left hand and arm swings downward is clearly a vital factor here, and I will be saying more about this later. For the moment, let's just remark that if it swings too fast, we do not have time to retain control, and "release" at the correct point. THIS IS WHY THE DOWNWARD SWING MUST BE SMOOTH AND EVEN. Indeed, it is true to say that THE SLOWER THE LEFT HAND AND ARM SWINGS DOWN INTO THE BALL THE MORE THE POWER THAT THE HANDS CAN DEVELOP. Why? Because the timing of the "release" can BE MORE PRECISE. Conversely, the faster the hand and arm swing the less precise the timing, and consequently the less the power developed.

Again, the simple action of banging in a nail with a hammer illustrates this point. The hand and arm doesn't move at lightning speed. If it did, timing, and consequently delivery of power, would be wrecked...that is if you succeed in hitting the nail at all! No, the hand and arm moves at moderate speed so that the hand and wrist can RETAIN CONTROL over the business of releasing power. Actually, the heavier the blow with the hammer, the slower the arm moves!

IT IS EXACTLY THE SAME IN THE GOLF SWING.

Hence, we see that a correctly timed release of power is the PRODUCT of a CORRECT START to the downswing with the left hand and arm. Given the correct start, the "angle" will be AUTO-MATICALLY MAINTAINED until the hands activate the release. I am not describing anything that is alien to human experience! A timed release is an instinctive skill . . . an action known to every human being, and employed almost daily in the course of normal work and play. It requires description in the golf swing only because many players are confused by incorrect information and advice.

Ben Hogan's "release" was most illuminating. His left hand and arm swung down at a slower speed than most players, yet his hands released the club-head faster and much later in the downswing than any other golfer that I have ever seen. He was a master of CONTROL AND TIMING. This gave him not only POWER, but also a certain knowledge of how far his ball would fly. He "released" at precisely the SAME POINT in each and every downswing, which gave him a STANDARD LENGTH OF SHOT with each club. This is the pinnacle of skill!

This matter of a standard "release point" in the swing has, to the best of my knowledge, never been discussed by golf theorists and teachers. Yet all the great players have it. It is the very ESSENCE of control . . . and incidentally ENJOYMENT . . . in striking a ball. Thus, beware of people who tell you to "hit early" or "hit late". This advice is meaningless. A properly timed release is WELL WITHIN YOUR CAPABILITY, and you should not . . . indeed CANNOT . . . settle for less!

123

SUMMARY

The hands and wrists ANTICI-PATE AND SENSE the "release" at the top of the swing ... and as the left hand and arm swings down. The downward swing of the left hand and arm then LOWERS THE HANDS into the release area, which is at about waist height. The shaft and club-head meanwhile have remained BEHIND THE HANDS because nothing has been done to alter the "angle". Now, with club-line through the ball ASSURED, the hands COMMENCE THE RE-LEASE and the club head ACCELERATES TO COME INTO LINE WITH THE HANDS AT THE MOMENT OF IMPACT. Or, put-ting it another way, the club-head, the shaft, and the hands are VERTICALLY ALIGNED AT IM-PACT, and the face of the club is DEAD SQUARE TO THE IN-TENDED LINE OF FLIGHT.

After impact, the left arm CON-TINUES TO SWING THROUGH THE HITTING AREA. It does not stop as the club-head catches up. It swings at UNIFORM SPEED THROUGHOUT THE DOWN-SWING, clear up to the finish.

Training will enable you to identify the "release point", and once you have it fixed, RETAIN IT. The combination of a STANDARDISED RELEASE POINT and GOOD CLUB LINE THROUGH THE BALL AT IM-PACT will produce shots of UNIFORM LENGTH and DEPEND-ABLE ACCURACY with each and every club. Further, you will achieve a swing in which THE LOWEST POINT OF THE ARC OCCURS JUST BEFORE, AND AFTER IM-PACT. No more "fat" and "topped" shots! It is this kind of mechanical consistency which produces good scores no matter what the conditions.

A correct backswing, a good top of the swing position, and above all the VITAL INTER-ACTION between the INSIDE OF THE LEFT FOOT AND THE HANDS at the top of the swing create the conditions for a suc-cessful downswing. Once achieve these conditions and a correct "conservation of power" and a "timed release" begin to take shape.

But we have run slightly ahead in the sequence. As soon as the left hand and arm started the downward swing THERE WAS A REACTION IN THE FEET AND LEGS. We must now consider this, and discover why it happens.

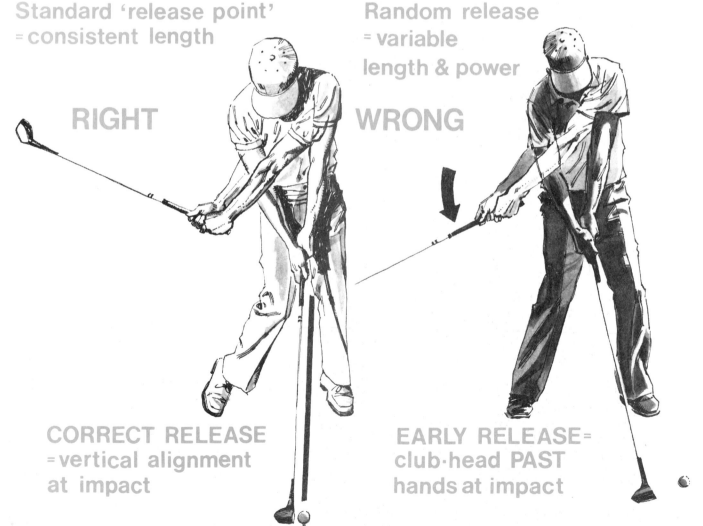

Standard 'release point'
= consistent length

Random release
= variable
length & power

RIGHT

WRONG

CORRECT RELEASE
= vertical alignment
at impact

EARLY RELEASE=
club·head PAST
hands at impact

THE DOWNSWING OCCURS FROM THE FEET . . . UP

I have already stressed the importance of "live feet" in the swing. I mentioned it in connection with the set-up and backswing. Now, we are going to see just how fundamentally important it is.

In the backswing the sequence of movement was (1) the left hand and arm STARTS the takeaway, (2) the shoulders begin to turn, (3) the right hip and side clears to the rear and (4) the left heel rises. This sequence enabled the left hand and arm to swing the club to a correct position at the top. Now, logically, in the downswing, WE REVERSE THAT SEQUENCE and we have (1) left hand and arm starts down and the body RESPONDS in the sequence (2) feet, (3) legs, (4) hips, and (5) shoulders last. NOTE THAT . . . SHOULDERS LAST!

The ⟩Lateral⟩ Shift⟩

Vital foot and
leg activity···its
PURPOSE in
the swing

125

The feet and legs set up a backward ˜resistance˜ which AMPLIFIES the POWER in the HANDS

Hence, no leg activity... vastly REDUCED POWER !

During the backswing the raising of the left heel both "charged the hands with power" at the top of the swing AND created the conditions for the "separation" of the left hand and arm from the body at the commencement of the downswing.

Now, in the downswing, as the hands "sense the release of the club-head", the left heel RESPONDS IMMEDIATELY BY RETURNING TO THE GROUND. The feet and legs are REACTING TO THE DOWNWARD SWING OF THE LEFT HAND AND ARM and the IMMINENT RELEASE OF POWER BY THE HANDS. This is the beginning of the "lateral shift".

Thus we can say that the "lateral shift" . . . or the movement that occurs in the feet and legs in a correct downswing . . . is a RESPONSE TO THE INTENTION TO DELIVER POWER WITH THE HANDS. Indeed, it occurs solely to RETAIN POWER IN THE HANDS FOR THE LONGEST POSSIBLE TIME. Let me explain.

In any human activity in which power or force is APPLIED WITH THE HANDS, a person FIRST ARRANGES HIS FEET AND BODY to enable that force to be applied.

In all sports involving the use of the HANDS, a player FIRST ARRANGES HIS FEET AND BODY TO MAKE THE APPLICATION OF FORCE BY THE HANDS EFFECTIVE. This holds good for boxing, tennis, cricket, baseball, tug-of-war, etc., etc. THE FEET AND BODY FIRST SET UP A FIRM BASE BEFORE POWER IS APPLIED BY THE HANDS.

THE SAME THING HAPPENS IN THE GOLF SWING.

Newton stated that "every action has an equal and opposite reaction". Thus, in order to exert a force in one direction (in this case, with the hands in the direction of the target), it is first necessary to set up a COUNTER FORCE or "RESISTANCE" in the OPPOSITE DIRECTION (away from the target). This is all that is happening in the "lateral shift".

A backward "resistance" is being set up in the lower body (below the waist) to ENABLE THE HANDS TO SWING POWER-FULLY INTO AND THROUGH IMPACT . . . AND THEN FLY POWERFULLY AWAY FROM THE BODY up into the follow through.

Thus, the "lateral shift" enables the HANDS to SWING POWER-FULLY from the point of "release" clear through impact and up into the finish.

We can go further and say that the strength of the "RESISTANCE" (or counter force) that is set up in the lower body DIRECTLY GOVERNS the amount of force that you can generate with the hands. Hence . . .

Little "resistance" . . . little force.

Great "resistance" . . . great force.

Thus, if you do not first SET UP THE NECESSARY "RESIST-ANCE" IN THE LOWER BODY YOU CANNOT GENERATE MAXIMUM POWER WITH THE HANDS. Or putting it in golfing terms, players who correctly use their feet and legs in the downswing generate power. Those who do not, hit weak shots.

Jack Nicklaus has a more pronounced "lateral shift" than any other player that I have ever seen. He thus sets up a massive "resistance" that ENABLES HIS HANDS TO DEVELOP CORRESPONDINGLY ENORMOUS POWER. This is perhaps why he asserts that his power "comes from his legs". I would rather say that his leg action, and the "resistance" that it provides, INCREASES THE POWER IN HIS HANDS AND ARMS . . . AND RETAINS IT THERE FOR AN EXCEPTIONALLY LONG TIME Hence his awesome power.

Conversely, we talk of veteran players in various sports whose "legs have gone". What we are saying, in effect, is that the legs no longer provide the "resistance" for a massive application of power BY THE HANDS. Hence, a re-duced performance is the result.

Thus, the AMOUNT OF POWER THAT CAN BE DEVELOPED BY THE HANDS is in direct proportion to the "RESISTANCE" that is set up in the FEET, LEGS, AND LOWER BODY. That is why "leg action" in the golf swing is essential for power. IT CREATES POWER IN THE HANDS.

In the process of performing the "lateral shift", the hips turn in the direction of the target. THIS IS AN ENTIRELY AUTOMATIC AND SUBCONSCIOUS ACTION. I only draw attention to it because it has been asserted for many years THAT THE DOWNSWING IS STARTED BY A TURN OF THE HIPS TOWARDS THE TARGET. This analysis is entirely wrong, as we have already seen. Please erase this concept entirely from your mind. It is perhaps the most destructive idea ever conceived in golf teaching.

I will explain later how it arose, and why so many great players wrongly assert that a hip turn STARTS THE DOWNSWING.

A hip turn, of course, does occur. But it is a PRODUCT of the intention to use the hands . . . DEFINITELY NOT THE CAUSE. It is really quite absurd to say that the hands are set in motion by hip movement. I know of no other sport in which this assertion is made. How can it then be true of golf?

Golf theorists have consistently made the mistake of asserting that EFFECTS are CAUSES . . . and have done a great deal of damage in the process! This is the most notorious example I can think of. Forget it . . . and the quicker you do so, the better!

No leg activity, reduced power !

EXERCISES
The "SWING AND STOP" exercise

To create a SQUARE IMPACT off the MIDDLE of the blade ··· and many other benefits ···

We have discussed the "release", and the correct impact position that is brought about when the "release" is correctly timed. The shoulders are square. The hands, club-shaft, and club-head are VERTICALLY ALIGNED AT THE MOMENT OF IMPACT, and the face of the club is SQUARE (at right angles) to the intended line of flight.

Here is an exercise that will help you to achieve these conditions at impact. Take an eight iron and go through your normal swing action, but STOP THE CLUB AT IMPACT. DO NOT GO THROUGH INTO THE FINISH!

Perform the swing, STOPPING the club at IMPACT...

1

2

4

6

3&5

CHECKLIST (Check against numbers on drawings)

Now check that your shoulders are square ... or better still in the pre-square position. Check that you have vertical alignment as described above, with the face of the club SQUARE. Also check the position of your legs. The right heel should be OFF THE GROUND.

Repeat this "swing and stop" exercise often. It brings many benefits. It (1) enables you to "standardise your point of re-lease". (2) You can check that the shoulders are remaining STILL at the beginning of the downswing so that proper "separation" of the left hand and arm is being achieved. (3) The SQUARENESS of the blade at impact can be checked. (4) The SQUARENESS of the shoulders at impact can be checked. (5) You can check that the ball is coming off the MIDDLE of the face or blade. (6) By repeating this exercise

often you can FEEL the importance of the "resistance".

Further, it establishes firmly the idea that THE SHOULDERS DO NOT TURN UNTIL AFTER THE BALL HAS BEEN STRUCK. If they turn BEFORE impact the alignment of the arms and hands relative to the intended line of flight MUST BE DESTROYED. The club-head MUST then move ACROSS the line of flight from out-to-in.

STOP

DON'T go into the follow-through (which involves a turn of the shoulders) until the SQUARE IMPACT has been perfected

The shoulders MUST be SQUARE at impact !

They turn into the 'open' position AFTER the ball has been struck, holding the 'line'

The shoulders turn into the "open" position AFTER IMPACT . . . and then only to ALLOW THE CLUB-HEAD TO REMAIN ON THE INTENDED LINE OF FLIGHT after impact, as they free-wheel up into the follow through and finish.

Do this exercise often while you are building a new swing. DO NOT GO INTO THE FOLLOW THROUGH until the impact position is PERFECT in every detail. ANY HINT OF SHOULDER OPENING PRIOR TO IMPACT IN THE DOWNSWING MUST BE ERASED FROM YOUR ACTION!

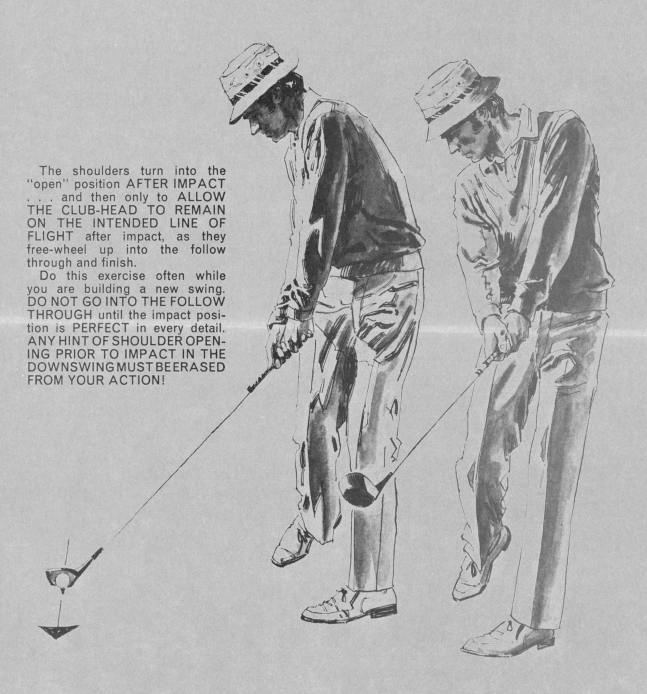

TEMPO · Key to the truly consistent swing. The means of retaining what you have learned

To achieve Tempo is to acquire the final polish to your swing action. Indeed, Tempo alone enables you to RETAIN ALL THAT I HAVE SAID ABOUT the swing. It is a MASTER REGULATOR of the entire system which, when acquired, enables the sequence to occur in the correct order, and with perfect timing. AND ALL THIS HAPPENS AUTOMATICALLY when Tempo has been built in!

Tempo is acquired by training. You condition yourself to perform the swing action that you have learned NO MATTER WHAT THE CONDITIONS. This conditioning process then supplants your "reflex" . . . your subconscious, involuntary instinct to develop power BEFORE IT IS REQUIRED . . . which ruins timing and swing shape.

Tempo not only brings these unruly impulses under control . . . it actually NEGATES THEM ALTOGETHER.

How do these "reflex" actions arise? The answer is the EYES stimulate these powerful reflexes! Unlike many other sports . . . tennis, cricket, football . . . a golfer has A LOT OF TIME to VISUALLY ASSESS his shot. He considers the DISTANCE and POWER required, wind, slope, lie, etc., etc. In doing all this, the poor player allows the idea of "power" to dominate his thinking. Indeed, even as he is playing his shot HIS MIND IS ON THE TARGET AREA rather than the job in hand! His sequence of priorities is WRONG, and consequently the SEQUENCE OF HIS SWING is equally wrong. He allows power to be developed at "any old place" in the swing . . . usually far TOO EARLY IN THE SEQUENCE! He has absolutely no Tempo, or control over the "power reflex".

The good player presents an entirely different approach. He considers his problem calmly, assessing power and distance, etc. BUT HIS ACQUIRED SENSE OF TEMPO GIVES HIM A FEELING OF WHERE, IN THE SWING SEQUENCE, THAT POWER WILL BE DEVELOPED. And further, he KNOWS that his controlled swing action WILL produce the required power . . . AT THE RIGHT TIME. That is, maximum club head acceleration will OCCUR AT THE BALL in each and every swing, giving uniform power and distance for every club in the bag! Hence, having assessed his shot and selected his club, his TEMPO GUARANTEES that POWER IS DEVELOPED IN THE RIGHT PLACE IN THE SEQUENCE, making for a shot of predictable length. That's what TEMPO means!

"Head up", or looking up before the ball has been struck is a matter of "reflex". It happens because POWER has been released EARLY, so the player looks up to see the result! Once power has gone, nothing on earth will prevent him from doing so. A good player never does this. His eyes remain on the ball . . . AWAITING THE RELEASE OF POWER . . . which occurs BETWEEN THE FEET. It is not a conscious action. He is still looking at the ball because power HAS NOT YET BEEN RELEASED. When it is released . . . at the right place . . . he looks up. A logical sequence of events.

, Hence, "Hit early . . . look early. Hit late . . . look late".

Tempo is a word that is often used in connection with the golf swing, but it is seldom defined. Swinging with tempo is SWINGING AT A SPEED WHICH ENABLES YOU TO BOTH RETAIN YOUR SWING "SHAPE" . . . AND RETAIN CONTROL OVER THE HANDS AT ALL TIMES. In other words, tempo and control are indivisible. We have been learning a new movement. Now we must perform the movement at a speed that will ENABLE US TO RETAIN CONTROL throughout. Hence "fast" and "slow" are negative terms. Faster or slower than what?

Here is an exercise that will resolve this question of "swing speed" for you. It also, incidentally, enables you to reinforce the feeling of "separation" of the left hand and arm from the body.

TEMPO EXERCISE

Assume the correct address position as described in Lesson 1 with both arms extended, palms facing each other. The distance between the hands is equal to the width of the shoulders. Now simply move both arms up together to just above head height . . . and down again. Repeat this up and down motion first without,

and then with a club in your hands.

THE SPEED AT WHICH YOU MOVE YOUR ARMS IN THIS EXERCISE IS THE SPEED AT WHICH YOU SHOULD SWING YOUR HANDS AND ARMS IN THE GOLF SWING ITSELF!

Note how smooth and easy this up/down action is. No effort is required. It is a genuine SWING of the hands and arms. THIS SMOOTHNESS AND FREEDOM MUST BE CARRIED OVER TO YOUR GOLF SWING. You must discipline yourself to swing the club AT THIS SAME SPEED in your golf swing.

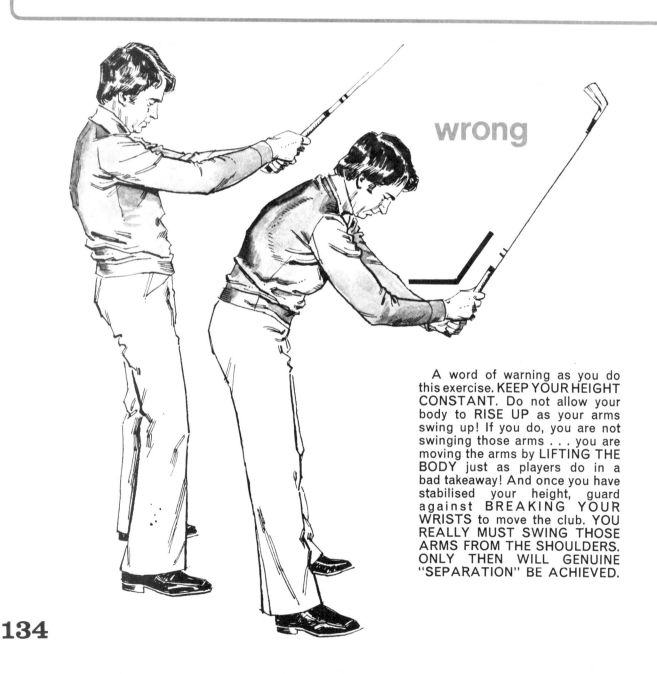

wrong

A word of warning as you do this exercise. KEEP YOUR HEIGHT CONSTANT. Do not allow your body to RISE UP as your arms swing up! If you do, you are not swinging those arms . . . you are moving the arms by LIFTING THE BODY just as players do in a bad takeaway! And once you have stabilised your height, guard against BREAKING YOUR WRISTS to move the club. YOU REALLY MUST SWING THOSE ARMS FROM THE SHOULDERS. ONLY THEN WILL GENUINE "SEPARATION" BE ACHIEVED.

Unless you can do this exercise, you cannot possibly achieve the "swing model". The arms MUST swing freely from the shoulder joints…

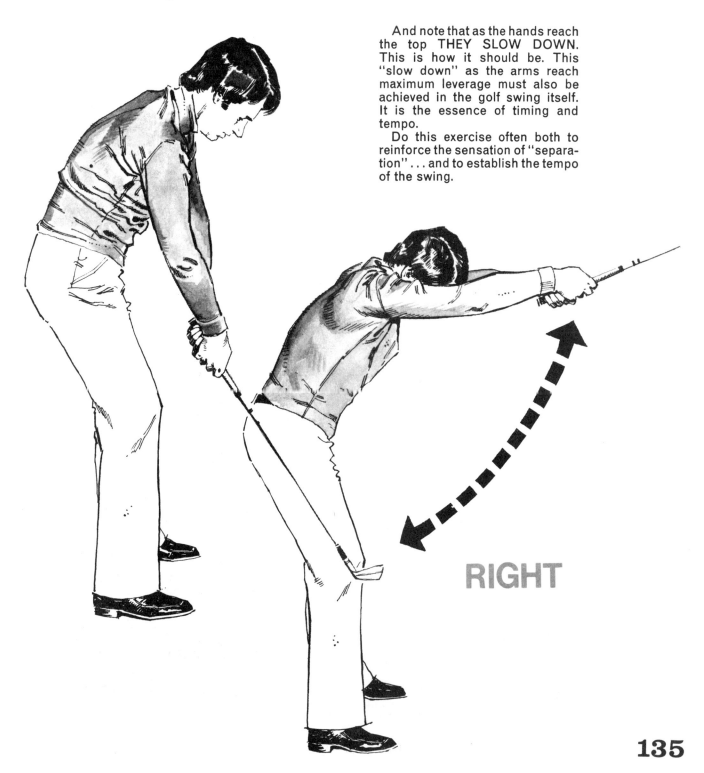

And note that as the hands reach the top THEY SLOW DOWN. This is how it should be. This "slow down" as the arms reach maximum leverage must also be achieved in the golf swing itself. It is the essence of timing and tempo.

Do this exercise often both to reinforce the sensation of "separation"… and to establish the tempo of the swing.

RIGHT

TEMPO, the ultimate refinement that concentrates POWER at exactly the right place ··· EVERY TIME you swing!

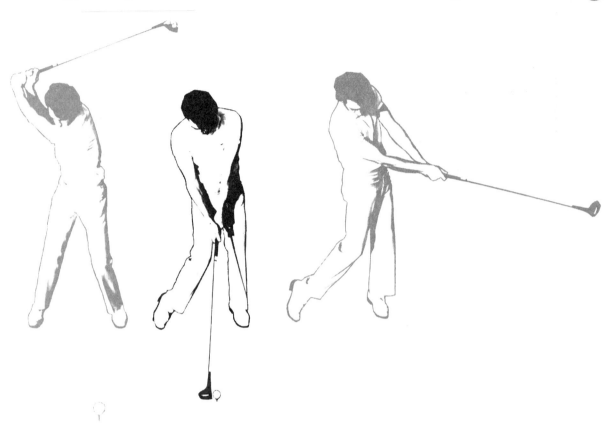

Thus, it becomes clear, as I said earlier, that to advise a player to "swing faster" or "slower" is meaningless. TEMPO is a matter of establishing the SPEED OF THE HAND AND ARM SWING THAT ALLOWS SUFFICIENT TIME FOR A SMOOTH TRANSITION FROM BACKSWING TO DOWNSWING, and once that is achieved, to swing down into the ball again allowing SUFFICIENT TIME TO "RELEASE" POWER WITH THE HANDS AND WRISTS AT THE CORRECT INSTANT OF TIME.

Why is this so important? We talked earlier about the absolute necessity of retaining the "swing shape" . . . that is, learning and REPEATING the correct swing movement. ONLY BY RETAINING A CONSTANT TEMPO CAN WE RETAIN A CONSTANT SWING

SHAPE. Indeed, tempo and swing shape are indivisible too! Distort tempo and the swing shape will vary . . . and vice versa.

I am reminded of Tony Jacklin's remark after he won the Open. He said "I had to keep on reminding myself to keep up my tempo". His tempo (speed of swing) was perfect, and he realised that as long as it remained CONSTANT he would continue to play well.

Further, if your tempo varies, your "release point" with the hands must also vary. Result, erratic length and inaccuracy. In a word . . . INCONSISTENCY.

TEMPO makes the difference between the golf champions and the rest of the pack. Tempo makes a player feel powerful. He senses that he has the time, and the control to develop maximum power at the ball. This is, inci-

dentally, what makes the game of golf enjoyable. Tempo alone creates this mechanical excellence that lasts through season after season . . . never varying. That is why the "swingers" ultimately outlast the "hitters" in big time golf. Why men like Snead, Littler, Boros, Casper and Faulkner still make golf look easy. THEY HAVE A CONSTANT TEMPO.

The conclusion therefore must be that most golfers SWING MUCH TOO FAST TO RETAIN CONTROL OVER THE DELIVERY. Consequently the "point of release" and the swing "shape" itself are subject to constant variation.

Swing shape and "point of delivery" cannot be standardised until a CONSTANT TEMPO has been achieved. You now know how to acquire it.

We have now traced through the entire downswing sequence from the "top" to the finish. At the finish, the body is in perfect balance with the chest squarely facing the target, and the hands alongside the head at about the level of the left ear. The arms are entirely free of tension, with both elbows pointing downward. The forearms thus resemble the two sides of a narrow-based triangle . . . not precisely vertical, but definitely not splayed out.

Control of this finish is held from the waist line and the firm left leg. The right knee is alongside the left and the right foot is up on the toe. This, too, is contributing to balance.

Club-face check at the finish

Or how to monitor every shot you make

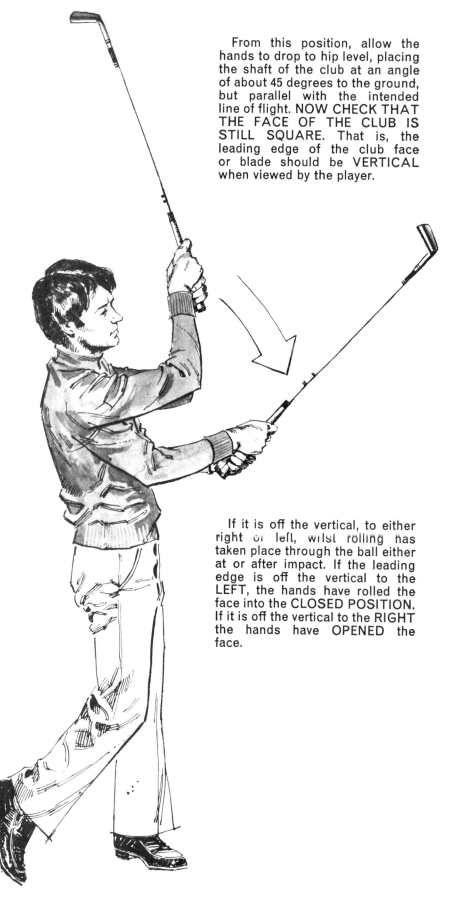

From this position, allow the hands to drop to hip level, placing the shaft of the club at an angle of about 45 degrees to the ground, but parallel with the intended line of flight. NOW CHECK THAT THE FACE OF THE CLUB IS STILL SQUARE. That is, the leading edge of the club face or blade should be VERTICAL when viewed by the player.

First, drop the hands to about waist high. Then make this check···

If it is off the vertical, to either right or left, wrist rolling has taken place through the ball either at or after impact. If the leading edge is off the vertical to the LEFT, the hands have rolled the face into the CLOSED POSITION. If it is off the vertical to the RIGHT the hands have OPENED the face.

At the finish of every stroke, the club·face should still be SQUARE. The leading edge should be vertical.

Note that I said AT OR AFTER IMPACT. Why be concerned about what happens after impact? The answer is that if the face is coming out of alignment after impact IT IS ONLY A MATTER OF TIME before it happens pre-impact. Further, errors of face alignment at and after impact CAN be sufficient to affect accuracy just that little bit.

The important thing is that the FACE MUST BE SQUARE AT THE FINISH. If it is coming out of alignment you must discover WHERE and WHEN.

If the face is not square at the finish check your position at the top (see Lesson 2, Page 77). If that is correct, refer to the "Swing and Stop" exercise in this lesson.

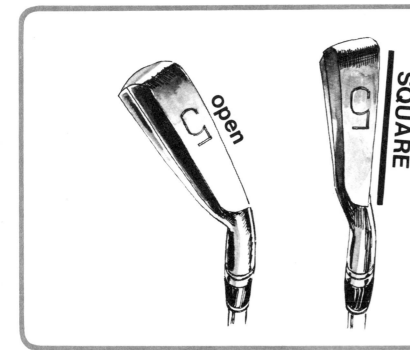

open   SQUARE

closed

139

The finish reveals a great deal. Generally speaking, a good player is flattish on the backswing and UPRIGHT IN THE FINISH. The poor player is upright in the backswing AND FLAT IN THE FINISH.

The former has achieved a club-line through the ball. The latter has not. His club has moved ACROSS THE LINE OF FLIGHT through impact, from out to in, which is evident in his spin type of finish.

Learn to analyse your shots by what happens at the finish. You will then soon begin to sense EXACTLY WHAT IS GOING ON IN YOUR SWING and know how to remedy errors.

POOR

high

flat

GOOD

flattish

high

The finish reveals how good, or bad, your club-line has been!

This is the ¯shape¯ you MUST ERASE, and here's how you do it···

A vital exercise

Here is an absolutely vital exercise that every golfer must master. Everything in this course of instruction depends upon your ability to do this exercise to perfection.

Its purpose is simple. It is designed to eliminate . . . once and for all . . . the dreadful "concave" body shape (illustrated) which is the cause of all that is bad in the golf swing.

This exercise can be performed anywhere, as you do not need a club in your hands to do it. Indeed, if you cannot do it WITHOUT A CLUB, you certainly will never master it with a club.

Every professional teacher should INSIST that this exercise is mastered by novices BEFORE they ever actually swing a club. If they did, it would save months of hard work. Experienced players too, should be introduced to it immediately. This exercise, more than anything else, has enabled me to transform players in less than two years, to championship and international class.
IT CONTAINS THE VERY ESSENCE OF A CORRECT SWING MOVEMENT. It absolutely MUST be mastered by all golfers of whatever ability.

Most players, as we have seen,

allow their bodies to "rise up" in the backswing as the club swings to the top. Again, in the downswing, they tend to move the club down from the top with "body propulsion" . . . rotating the shoulders through the ball as they do so. They end up with a flat, "round" type of finish with the shaft of the club pointing to the left of the target.

Here is an exercise designed to eliminate these errors. I introduced it to many top amateur players at Muirfield in 1974. They were delighted with it and said that it gave them an entirely new "feel" of the swing.

141

The entire swing action in a single exercise! You don't even need a club to do it, but you MUST perform it to PERFECTION with the aid of a mirror.

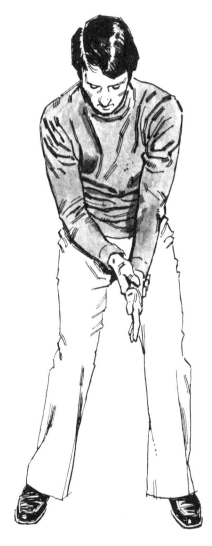

Adopt the normal address position, and with the left shoulder "up", grasp the extended left arm around the wrist with the right hand.

Now perform the backswing by swinging the left hand and arm to the top as described in Lesson 2.

If you fail to master it ···
all else simply won't slot into place !

Be sure to make it a free swing with the left shoulder "up". Keep the weight "down" as the left hand and arm swings up. Feel that the arm is swinging to MAXIMUM LEVERAGE.

This exercise will help you to sense that the body turns to PERMIT A FREE SWING OF THE LEFT HAND AND ARM. You will also feel the need to RAISE THE LEFT HEEL in order to achieve maximum leverage. Remember, the left foot must "break" AT THE TOE JOINTS. There must be no inward roll of the left foot. And the RIGHT KNEE REMAINS FLEXED, just as it was at address.

Performing this exercise makes us realise that a responsive and perfectly balanced body ENABLES THE LEFT HAND AND ARM TO SWING FULLY AND FREELY. It also places the arms in a correct position at the top.

At the top, the shoulders are fully turned, AND REMAIN SO AS THE DOWNSWING BEGINS. We then swing the left hand and arm down into the ball NOTING THAT THE "LATERAL SHIFT" OCCURS AS A RESULT OF THIS DOWNWARD SWING.

As the loft hand enters the "release area" the right foot and knee "kicks in" to the shot just as we described in the item on the "lateral shift".

The left hand and arm then moves INTO AND ALONG THE INTENDED LINE OF FLIGHT through impact, causing the shoulders to TURN AFTER IMPACT to allow the left hand and arm to swing freely up into the finish.

In short, this exercise contains THE VERY ESSENCE OF THE ENTIRE SWING MOVEMENT, and can be performed anywhere, without a golf club to hand. It REINFORCES ALL THE POINTS that I have been making about a correct swing action.

Perform this exercise often, standing in front of a mirror. Compare your body position with these illustrations and make sure you have every detail perfect. Repeat the exercise until it becomes automatic.

Above all, it teaches you to perform the body turn WITHOUT ALLOWING THE BODY TO ASSUME A ''CONCAVE'' SHAPE (see LESSON 2, Page 85). If you cannot achieve a correct ''CONVEX'' body shape without a club in your hands, you certainly will not be able to do it with a club!

This exercise is the FOUNDATION of your new swing, transforming this⋯

into THIS

BACKSWING «MASTER SEQUENCE»

1

A correct set-up is a vital prelude to a correct backswing. The set-up is simply an arrangement of the body that permits a free swing of the left hand and arm. That is all.

2

A backward movement of the left hand and arm *creates* the initial club-head movement. Note that the shoulders have hardly moved at all! It is *after* this initial movement that the shoulders must begin their turn to enable the arm swing to continue freely.

Tempo and control

We have examined the backswing step by step. We now know the *purpose* of the backswing and *how* it is carried out.

Now we see the movement as a whole, and we see our concepts in action. We have progressed a little bit at a time . . . stage by stage . . . because each phase, if carried out correctly *creates the conditions* for correctly carrying out the subsequent phases. Equally, error at any stage is carried over into the next stage.

Now we see the whole backswing movment as one fluid, strain-free action. We see in action the principle that the left hand and arm *swings* the club and the body *responds* to this swinging movement by turning in a controlled, "shaped" manner to *assist* and make possible this swing of the left hand and arm.

Once the basic correct movements are grasped the backswing is simple to carry out. Our object must be to perfect the correct movement until it is automatic . . . subconscious.

Above all, remember we are not trying to hit the ball on the backswing. We are merely *positioning* ourselves for the downward swing of the club. Smoothness, ease of effort, and above all *control* are the watchwords here. Think about "hitting" and tension will destroy the free swing . . . the body will take over and the "shape" of the backswing will be ruined.

You are *training* the body to move in response to the arm swing.

Forget the ball! Control the impulse to "hit" and your backswing will become the foundation of a sound, controlled swing.

Without a controlled backswing . . . you're nowhere!

At the top. Right side fully cleared to the rear. Left heel up. Shoulders fully turned. Left shoulder "up." This "shaped" body movement has permitted the left hand and arm to swing the club into a correct position at the top. This means that the arm and hand has swung to its MAXIMUM LEVERAGE, placing the club correctly on the swing plane. The body has *responded* in a controlled manner to assist, and not hinder, this swing. That is the sole role of the body. It never, never *causes* the movement of the hand and arm. Rather, it makes possible this swing by turning correctly. THIS MUST BE UNDERSTOOD. It is absolutely vital!

6

3

The shoulder turn has started. The left hand and arm is *swinging* the club backwards and upwards so the left shoulder remains "up." It is when the body moves the club that the left shoulder dips down! Now the right hip begins to move back in *response* to the shoulder turn, but the right leg has retained the same *flexed* position that it had at address. The body is *responding* to the *swing* of the left hand and arm.

5

Almost there! The "shaped" body turn has permitted the left hand and arm to swing freely from the shoulder. Hence, the left shoulder has not dipped down . . . it has maintained its height from the ground. The clearance of the right side has enabled the shoulder turn to go ahead unrestricted. The left heel is "up." The flexed right leg is holding everything in check. Note that the knees and hips are still virtually horizontal. No swaying here!

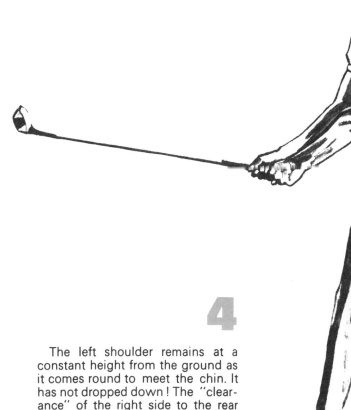

4

The left shoulder remains at a constant height from the ground as it comes round to meet the chin. It has not dropped down! The "clearance" of the right side to the rear continues, to enable the shoulders to turn *fully*. The entire turn is being dictated by the progress of the left hand and arm. Now, the player feels the need to raise the left heel so that a *full* body turn can continue. The head remains still.

DOWNSWING "MASTER SEQUENCE"

We have said that CONTROL OF THE SHOULDERS is the key to a successful downswing. This control assures two vital factors. (1) We can achieve "separation". That is, a GENUINE DOWNWARD SWING of the left hand and arm can take place as a preliminary to a POWERFUL RELEASE BY THE HANDS AND WRISTS. (2) We can maintain the desired CLUB-LINE DOWN INTO THE BALL which results in an impact along the intended line of flight.

WITHOUT SHOULDER CONTROL, NEITHER OF THESE FACTORS CAN OCCUR.

Shoulder control is achieved by CORRECT FOOT AND LEG ACTION. The pressure felt under the big toe joint of the left foot when a player is at the top ENABLES HIM TO MOMENTARILY HOLD THE SHOULDERS IN THE FULLY TURNED POSITION as the downward swing of the left hand and arm gets under way.

After that, the movement of the FEET, LEGS, AND HIPS in the "lateral shift" . . . a shift of the LOWER BODY IN THE DIRECTION OF THE TARGET . . . facilitates CONTINUED CONTROL OF THE SHOULDERS.

This is why I say that in the the downswing, THE BODY UNWINDS FROM THE FEET . . . UP. After the initial downward swing of the left hand and arm, the feet and legs REACT IMMEDIATELY unwinding in the sequence FEET, LEGS, HIPS, SHOULDERS. NOTE THAT . . . SHOULDERS LAST. Thus, proper control of the shoulders DEPENDS UPON CORRECT LEG ACTION.

One thing is sure. IF THE FEET AND LEGS ARE INACTIVE AND DEAD, THE SHOULDERS ARE BOUND TO TURN FROM THE TOP. Nothing can stop them from doing so. If movement occurs in the lower body, THE UPPER BODY CAN BE CONTROLLED. If the lower body is inactive, the upper body (shoulders) MUST DO THE WORK. IT IS A CLEAR CHOICE BETWEEN ONE OR THE OTHER.

Thus, the downswing is a movement in which the lower body (below the waist) is ALWAYS TURNING AHEAD OF THE UPPER BODY. The axis of the hips TURNS AHEAD of the axis of the shoulders. Indeed, while perfecting this movement, a player must CONSCIOUSLY HOLD BACK HIS SHOULDERS as this lower body activity takes place. The shoulders RESIST the turn in the lower body UNTIL IMPACT HAS OCCURRED. Then, they turn to ALLOW THE HANDS AND ARMS TO CONTINUE TO SWING AWAY FROM THE BODY, out in the direction of the target, keeping the club-head ON THE INTENDED LINE OF FLIGHT AS THEY DO SO.

This resistance of the shoulders to the turn in the lower body is a vital skill WHICH YOU ABSOLUTELY MUST ACQUIRE. It is clearly evident in the downswings of all great players, past and present.

However, I must state most emphatically that this movement in the lower body (the "lateral shift") DOES NOT SET THE HANDS AND ARMS IN MOTION. It occurs in RESPONSE to the downward swing of the HANDS.

Now let's examine the downswing in detail, bearing these points very firmly in mind.

PICTURE 1

We are at the top. The left heel is RAISED. The pressure felt under the INSIDE (big toe joint) of the left foot is providing an UPWARD resistance . . . a system of control that ENALBES A PLAYER TO MOMENTARILY HOLD THE SHOULDERS IN THE FULLY TURNED POSITION as the downward swing of the left hand and arm gets under way. Further, this UPWARD resistance POWERS THE HANDS as they begin to swing down. Without it the upper left arm would have no LEVERAGE. Thus, the means of controlling the shoulders is ESTABLISHED BEFORE THE DOWNSWING BEGINS by the UPWARD resistance from the ball of the LEFT FOOT. Now, the intention to deliver power with the hands and wrists INITIATES THE DOWNWARD SWING OF THE LEFT HAND AND ARM.

PICTURE 2

As soon as the downward swing of the left hand and arm gets under way THE LEFT HEEL RETURNS TO THE GROUND, and the "lateral shift" commences. The body begins to "unwind" from the FEET . . . UP, while the shoulders RESIST this unwinding process. The feet and knees, especially the left foot, are providing UPWARD PRESSURE as the hands and left arm swing down. Again, force and counter force, which makes for power. Note that the "resistance" is being established in the LEFT FOOT AND LEG, but the right foot is now becoming active.

WARNING! THE HANDS AND WRISTS ARE IN CONTROL AT ALL TIMES while the left hand and arm makes the downward swing. The right arm and elbow, however, is ENTIRELY PASSIVE PRIOR TO IMPACT. It literally does nothing! If the right arm is allowed to come into the swing too early THE CLUB WILL BE THROWN FORWARD to an "outside" line which will wreck the direction of the swing. You should not be conscious of the contribution of the right arm (as opposed to the hand and wrist which ARE ACTIVE AT ALL TIMES) in the stroke until you are WELL INTO THE FOLLOW THROUGH (Pictures 5 and 6).

RECAP ON THE ADDRESS POSITION

Now that we have described the entire downswing sequence in detail, and we understand what happens . . . and WHY it happens, let's return briefly to the address to note that the conditions for the "resistance" that we have been talking about originated right there.

A correct address position creates a correct impact position, in which the resistance can operate to maximum effect.

At address, you will recall, we bent the body FORWARD FROM THE WAIST over FLEXED KNEES, with the buttocks protruding slightly. The angle of the back thus established placed the body in a correct position for the "resistance" to be effective at and after impact.

If you stand too upright at impact . . . and I warned you against this in Lesson 1 . . . you cannot use your legs correctly, and therefore you cannot set up any "resistance" in the downswing. Hence, your swing will lack power . . . and direction.

Only if the address position is correct, with the body bending forward correctly, can a player use his legs to set up the "resistance" in his back which creates the conditions for a free forward swing of the hands and arms, which results in a powerful and well directed follow-through.

Hence, a correct address position is vital to a powerful, controlled downswing. Without it, the legs cannot operate correctly to set up the "resistance" that gives the swing power.

MASTER SEQUENCE SUMMARY

That is the downswing sequence in essence. I have explained it in detail, stage by stage, so that the chain of events can be followed through. I NATURALLY DO NOT EXPECT YOU TO RETAIN ALL THIS INFORMATION IN YOUR HEAD. You simply don't need to. I am simply attempting to show how the hand and arm swing, the "release", and the "lateral shift" all DOVETAIL TOGETHER to produce a powerful, well directed swing ALONG THE INTENDED LINE OF FLIGHT.

The three main events of the downswing, the SWING of the left hand and arm, the LATERAL SHIFT in the lower body and the RELEASE with the hands are inter-related in the sequence.

Above all, I want to leave you with this conclusion about the downswing. We have seen that the "hip turn" occurs as part and parcel of the "lateral shift". It happens as the "resistance" is transferred from the legs to the small of the back AFTER IMPACT. Its purpose is to provide a counter force as the hands and arms fly away from the body in the follow through, and thus it contributes to the creation of power, and incidentally, BALANCE.

Thus, the "lateral shift" and the hip turn associated with it occur to set up the "resistance" that powers the hands through impact.

I say yet again. The hip turn DOES NOT set the hands and arms in motion at the beginning of the downswing!

The purpose of this MASTER SEQUENCE is to place the events of the downswing IN THE COR-RECT ORDER. The hip turn, as you have seen, occurs relatively late in the sequence. Traditional teaching has wrongly placed it at the BEGINNING of the sequence! THIS ERROR HAS CAUSED GOLFERS ENDLESS TROUBLE!

WARNING! THE WRISTS DO NOT ROLL THROUGH IMPACT. This incorrect idea is widely advocated and is the cause of much inaccuracy. At impact, the hands, wrists and arms are in EXACTLY THE SAME RELATIONSHIP TO THE BODY AS THEY WERE AT ADDRESS. When the shoulders turn AFTER IMPACT this relationship remains unchanged. Thus, no wrist or forearm rolling occurs at all. If the blade closes at, or after impact it will only be a matter of time before this happens prior to impact!

PICTURES 5 AND 6

Prior to impact the job of setting up the "resistance" had been done mainly by the feet and legs. Now, after impact, as the hands and arms PASS THE BODY, the "resistance" passes to the small of the back. Now the small of the back quickly "moves in" to set up the counter force to the swing of the hands and arms in the direction of the target. In so doing the "hip turn" occurs. Thus, the body is still RESPONDING to the SWING OF THE HANDS AND ARMS. It is turning simply to allow the hands and arms to swing freely up into the finish.

By setting up the "resistance" in this way the body MAINTAINS ITS HEIGHT through impact. We now see the importance of a correct address. The rump is pushed out and back as we bend forward from the waist, at address. This positions the body IN READINESS for the small of the back to become active AFTER IMPACT as just described. A straight, upright back at address is a weak position as it cannot lead to the creation of "resistance" after impact.

PICTURE 7

Finish. Correct foot and leg action has created a position of perfect balance, which is held from the waist line . . . up. The hands have "free wheeled" up to a high finish and have come to rest beside the left ear. Note that the sole of the right foot is now VERTICAL and balanced on the toe . . . evidence of proper leg action and a correct build up of the "resistance". There is a clear impression of POWER HAVING BEEN DELIVERED ALONG A LINE.

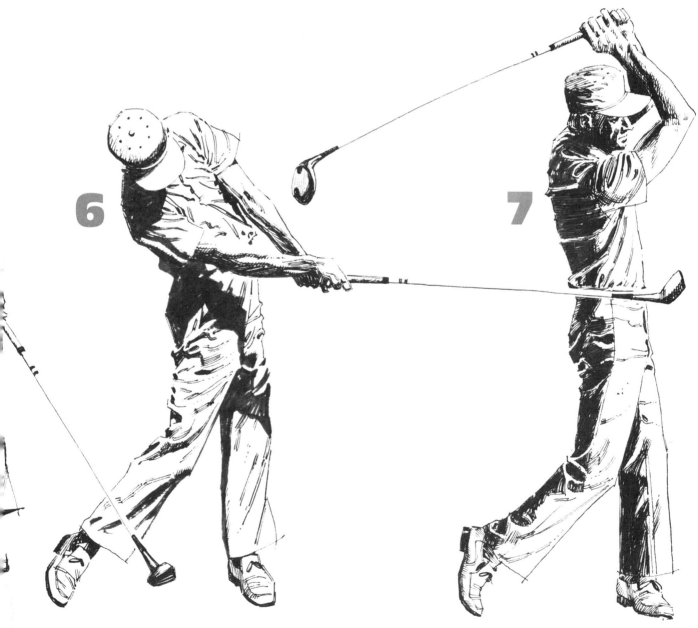

PICTURE 3

The hands and wrists have been anticipating the "release of power" right from the top . . . AND NOW THIS RELEASE BEGINS. Thus, the angle formed by the shaft and the left arm BEGINS TO INCREASE. The shoulders are still RESISTING the turn in the lower body. The right leg is now becoming active because the "resistance" is being transferred from the LEFT foot to the RIGHT foot. It is moving BACKWARDS as the downward swing of the hands and left arm becomes a HORIZONTAL swing through impact. This foot and leg activity is CREATING THE BACKWARD "RESISTANCE" that will RETAIN POWER IN THE HANDS AND WRISTS THROUGH IMPACT.

As the "release" of power by the hands and wrists takes place, the movement in the lower body . . . the leg activity . . . occurs REALLY FAST in order to establish the "resistance" BEFORE IMPACT TAKES PLACE. This means that the hands will be powerful at impact. A sluggish "lateral shift" serves no purpose at all, and makes for weak shots.

PICTURE 4

IMPACT! Just BEFORE the club arrives in the impact area the "resistance" is transferred to the BIG TOE JOINT OF THE RIGHT FOOT, and the right heel is now WELL CLEAR OF THE GROUND. The right knee has begun to fold in towards the left to create the conditions for the TRANSFER OF THE "RESISTANCE" TO THE SMALL OF THE BACK JUST AFTER IMPACT, where it will remain until the finish of the stroke.

The hands, club-shaft, and club-head are in VERTICAL ALIGNMENT at the moment of impact. The shoulders are SQUARE to the intended line of flight or, better still, in the pre-square position. This ensures that the club-face will remain SQUARELY on the intended line of flight through impact providing a SUSTAINED CONTACT with the ball, driving it forward.

We now see why CONTROL OF THE SHOULDERS is so important . . . and they CONTINUE TO RESIST the unwinding of the lower body EVEN AT IMPACT. This shoulder control, incidentally, is what "keeps the head still".

Origin of an error...

In the early days of golf the analysts thought and talked only of "swinging the club". A wristy, round the body swing was the ideal. Then it was realised that the body clearly had a lot to do with the movement. The pendulum abruptly swung the other way and the emphasis was placed on body action. The hands were said to be passive, and the idea that the hands are set in motion by body action arose . . . and has persisted to this day.

The truth lies between these two extremes. And the factor that links and unifies the extremes is THE SWING OF THE ARMS. IT HAS NEVER BEEN REALISED THAT A PLAYER HAS A PAIR OF ARMS TO SWING!

The role of the body is to allow the arms to swing to MAXIMUM LEVERAGE in the backswing. And in the downswing, the body sets up the conditions for a POWERFUL FORWARD DRIVE WITH THE HANDS AND ARMS. Thus the link between POWERFUL USE OF THE HANDS and correct body action is THE FREE SWING OF THE ARMS.

This is the area of golf theory that has been neglected, and has given rise to error in golf teaching.

I know that most of the world's top players have asserted that the "hip turn sets the hands in motion in the downswing". I have suggested an alternative concept.

I think this incorrect concept has arisen in the following way. First, as I have already said, there is currently an over emphasis on "body action" in golf teaching. This over emphasis has come from the books and instructional articles of the great players themselves. The reason for this is not difficult to discover.

I have told you about the "resistance" that is established in the lower body that makes possible a powerful swing of the hands and arms through impact. Top players are, quite naturally, EXTREMELY CON-SCIOUS of this movement in the lower body in the downswing. They have sensed, quite correctly, that it has an important bearing on the generation of power.

These top players, as I have already said, set up a really massive "resistance" in the feet, legs and body, which accounts for their enormous power. They also begin to set up this "resistance" MUCH EARLIER in the downswing movement than do average players. Hence, they mistakenly assume THAT THE BEGINNING OF THE "LATERAL SHIFT" IS THE BEGINNING OF THE DOWNSWING ITSELF. This leads quite naturally to the conclusion that "the hip turn sets the hands in motion at the beginning of the downswing".

One error has given rise to a second, more serious error.

The fact is that ONE IMPORTANT ELEMENT has been LEFT OUT of their analysis. It is the INITIAL DOWNWARD MOVEMENT OF THE LEFT HAND AND ARM WHILE THE SHOULDERS MOMENTARILY REMAIN IN THE FULLY TURNED POSITION AT THE BEGINNING OF THE DOWNSWING. Or the "separation", as I call it.

This is what TRIGGERS and CAUSES the "lateral shift". IT IS NOT THE OTHER WAY AROUND!

Golf theorists have, incredibly, not realised that A PLAYER HAS A PAIR OF ARMS TO SWING! Yet this is, in fact, THE FUNDAMENTAL BASIS OF THE ENTIRE GOLF ACTION. Everything else is secondary to that basic element.

Once this vital truth has been grasped, real and rapid progress can begin.

Curiously enough the American sport of Baseball provides the final proof of what I have been saying. The act of swinging a baseball bat is almost IDENTICAL to the golf action except, of course, that the striking implement swings on a different plane.

The Baseball player clearly FIRST SETS UP THE "RESISTANCE" IN THE LOWER BODY and then he SWINGS THE HANDS AND ARMS . . . and "releases" the bat with the hands and wrists to strike the ball, just as a golfer does.

Thus, the "resistance" has clearly POWERED THE HANDS AND ARMS . . . AND RETAINED POWER IN THE HANDS THROUGHOUT THE "STRIKE".

No baseball coach, to my knowledge, states that the foot, leg and hip activity ACTUALLY SETS THE HANDS AND ARMS IN MOTION! It would be absurd to say this AS IT CLEARLY DOES NOT HAPPEN THAT WAY!

Why, then, has this obvious error been made in golf teaching?

BECAUSE THE FUNDAMENTAL IMPORTANCE OF THE SWING OF THE HANDS AND ARMS HAS NEVER BEEN FULLY APPRECIATED IN GOLF TEACHING.

As I said in lesson 2, the body stays DOWN as the hands and arms SWING UP in the backswing. This is "resistance" . . . force and counter force.

Then, at the top, the UPWARD PRESSURE from the left big toe joint provides the point of "resistance" against which the left hand and arm can SWING DOWN POWERFULLY. Again, force and counter force.

Thus, the "resistance" in the golf swing is effective BEFORE THE DOWNSWING ACTUALLY BEGINS. It is only when the left hand and arm begins to SWING DOWN that the "resistance" becomes visually apparent as foot, leg and hip movement.

This is why I insist that the downward swing of the left hand and arm CAUSES the "lateral shift" and the hip turn. NOT THE OTHER WAY AROUND!

Consciously turning the hips to start the downswing can only result in opening the shoulders, which destroys the entire action.

A COURSE SUMMARY

We have now examined the entire golf swing in detail. I have given you my analysis of what happens, and I have given you the concepts that constitute my teaching method.

As I said right at the beginning, may of these concepts will be entirely new to you as they directly contradict "established ideas". You cannot be expected to grasp them all immediately. You will have to read, digest, and begin to understand them over a period of time. Of one thing I can assure you, THIS IS A PROVEN METHOD. I am not offering my ideas as suggestions that may help you. I KNOW THAT THIS ANALYSIS OF THE GOLF SWING, AND THE TEACHING METHOD THAT IS BASED UPON IT PRODUCES BETTER GOLFERS.

I offer you no gimmicks, no "cures" for hooks and slices. Quite simply, if you habitually hook or slice you can be sure that your swing is basically unsound. It is quite futile to give you a "cure" for the slice that will ultimately become a hook. I simply don't believe in such therapy. In order to play good, rewarding golf you MUST HAVE A SOUND METHOD. That is what I have given you here.

I stress again, this is not a theoretical exercise that may possibly improve your game. There is no trial and error about it. IT IS A SYSTEMATIC PRO-GRAMME FOR THE BUILDING OF A SOUND SWING which has produced many champions and low handicap players. You will not be able to apply all of its principles at once. But as you incorporate its elements into your swing your golf will begin to improve. Above all, it serves as a central reference point . . . A SWING MODEL . . . to which you can return at any time to check your action and refresh your memory on points of detail.

VARIATIONS IN STYLES

Some people may argue that many of the great players employ styles and mannerisms that do not accord with my analysis. My answer is that a MINORITY of top players do show differences of style, particularly in the back-swing. BUT THEY RETURN TO THE MODEL THAT I HAVE DESCRIBED BEFORE THE DOWN SWING BEGINS. Further, even these players with highly personal mannerisms deviate only margin-ally from the "model" that I have outlined in this course. They employ it for at least 70% of the time.

However, I contend that the VAST MAJORITY of top players, past and present, employ the "model" I have given you, and it is particularly evident in those WHO HAVE REMAINED AT THE TOP LONGER THAN THE REST.

THE MEASURE OF A GOLFER

What is the true measure of a golfer's ability? The answer is, THE QUALITY OF HIS WORST SHOTS. The worst shots of world class players are never so bad that they drop strokes wholesale. This is why they are consistent year in, year out.

The essence of professionalism in any sport (or other activity) is that YOUR MINIMUM STAND-ARD OF PERFORMANCE IS EXTREMELY HIGH. In golf, this is quite impossible with an un-sound action.

When I take my pupils out for a round of golf I am frankly NOT IMPRESSED by their best shots. IT IS THEIR WORST SHOTS THAT REMAIN IN MY MIND, for these are the shots THAT WILL RUIN THEIR SCORES and put them out of the running on payday.

In order to score well . . . consistently . . . YOU MUST HAVE A SOUND ACTION. Then your worst shots will be only marginally off line. Only sustained training based upon a SOUND SWING METHOD can produce the consistency that results in respectable scores ALL OF THE TIME.

NO PROFESSIONAL, OR TOP AMATEUR PLAYER CAN AFFORD TO SETTLE FOR LESS! One can stand on the first tee at any pro. tournament and watch a procession of hopeless swings. Such players may turn in the occasional good round, or even win the occasional tourna-ment. But they will never achieve the consistency that carries one to world class. Frankly, the swing action of the average professional player is basically no better than that of the competent amateur. The run of the mill pro. scores better because he plays more golf, putts better, and has superior hand action. I am often shocked by the swing actions of many young pros. who come to my school. They are simply making the best of what little they've got! But once they have been given a sound method they improve rapidly, and begin to gain confi-dence.

My purpose in devising this course of instruction was to correct certain errors in golf teaching, and thus enable players to progress more rapidly. Here, then, are the key new concepts that I have introduced in these lessons. They are "new" only because they have not been expressed IN THIS PARTICULAR WAY BEFORE. They are "old" in that the actual movements that I have described have been employed by all top golfers in my lifetime at least, and I have watched most of them!

ADDRESS

The address position (and the "set" of the arms) is dictated entirely by the intention to SWING THE HANDS AND ARMS. A correct address position ANTICIPATES and makes possible a correct position at impact, in which the "resistance" can play its proper part.

BACKSWING

The HANDS AND ARMS make the INITIAL MOVEMENT in the backswing, just as they do in the downswing. The shoulder turn then ENABLES the hands and arms to SWING FREELY TO MAXIMUM LEVERAGE at the top.

The concept of the "one piece takeaway" is therefore incorrect, as it depends upon a TURN OF THE SHOULDERS TO SET THE HANDS AND ARMS IN MOTION. This is, in fact, "body propulsion" . . . and is precisely what we are trying to avoid. The correct backswing movement takes the club to the top ON A CORRECT LINE, and positions the club correctly in readiness for the downward swing. THE BACKSWING IS NOT PERFORMED TO "GENERATE POWER".

Key points of the METHOD···

DOWNSWING

Power ORIGINATES in the HANDS AND WRISTS . . . and will be retained there ONLY IF THE FEET AND LEGS function correctly in the downswing, creating the "resistance" (backward counter-force) that is necessary for a powerful hand and arm swing through impact.

The intention to "release" this power in the hands and wrists CAUSES the downward swing of the left hand and arm which is the BEGINNING of the downswing. This momentary "separation" at the start of the downswing (as the shoulders remain fully turned) is the key to a correct start.

This downward swing then IMMEDIATELY TRIGGERS A REACTION IN THE FEET AND LEGS, which is the beginning of the "lateral shift". This lower body movement occurs solely TO RETAIN POWER IN THE HANDS AT ALL TIMES.

Thus, the "hip turn" DOES NOT START THE DOWNSWING as is so often claimed. If it does, the shoulders will "open" and "body propulsion" is again taking place which will destroy both club-line and a timed release.

THE BODY DOES NOT PROPEL (cause the movement of) THE HANDS AND ARMS AT ANY TIME. This is the golden rule.

IMPACT

The "resistance" (which is located in the small of the back just after impact) provides the backward counter-force that POWERS THE HANDS AND ARMS as they swing through impact and beyond . . . holding the club-head firmly ON THE LINE OF FLIGHT as they do so.

This is the secret of ACCURACY and POWER.

FINISH

A correct downswing creates a CONTROLLED, BALANCED FINISH. The finish (and the "club face check" at the end of each stroke) is an INFALLIBLE RECORD of what has gone before. Errors in the finish point to errors in the swing itself. Discover where they are occurring.

The good golfer KNOWS exactly WHERE his club must be at any given time, and HOW to place it there. That's Method! Anything less is pure guesswork !

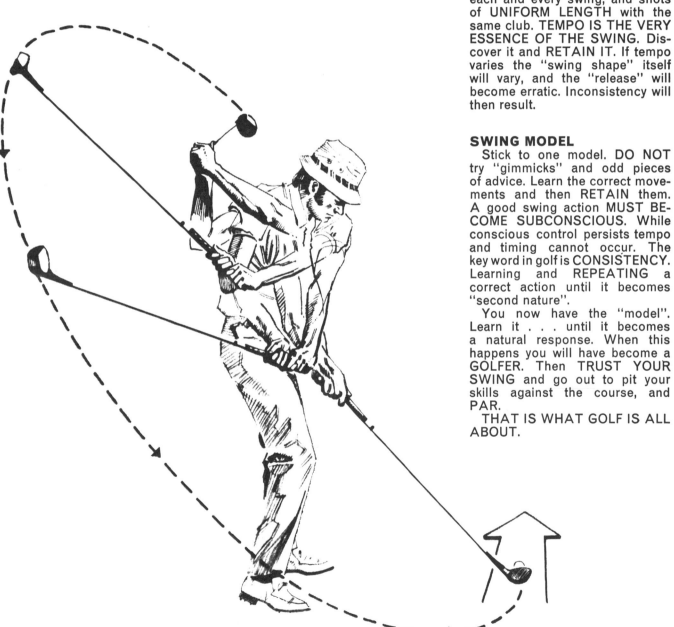

CLUB-LINE

A correct swing movement creates DIRECTION and POWER. The "shaped swing" brings about good club-line AUTOMATICALLY . . . assuring an impact INTO AND ALONG THE INTENDED LINE OF FLIGHT in each and every stroke.

TEMPO

The priceless art of GIVING YOURSELF TIME in which to make a powerful and correctly controlled delivery of power with the hands and wrists.

Once acquired, it leads to a "standardised release point" in each and every swing, and shots of UNIFORM LENGTH with the same club. TEMPO IS THE VERY ESSENCE OF THE SWING. Discover it and RETAIN IT. If tempo varies the "swing shape" itself will vary, and the "release" will become erratic. Inconsistency will then result.

SWING MODEL

Stick to one model. DO NOT try "gimmicks" and odd pieces of advice. Learn the correct movements and then RETAIN them. A good swing action MUST BECOME SUBCONSCIOUS. While conscious control persists tempo and timing cannot occur. The key word in golf is CONSISTENCY. Learning and REPEATING a correct action until it becomes "second nature".

You now have the "model". Learn it . . . until it becomes a natural response. When this happens you will have become a GOLFER. Then TRUST YOUR SWING and go out to pit your skills against the course, and PAR.

THAT IS WHAT GOLF IS ALL ABOUT.